ANOTHER DAY,
ANOTHER DOLLAR

The
Civilian Conservation Corps
in the Catskills

DIANE GALUSHA

BLACK·DOME

Published by
Black Dome Press Corp.
1011 Route 296, Hensonville, New York 12439
www.blackdomepress.com   tel: (518) 734-6357

First Edition Paperback 2009

ISBN-13: 978-1-883789-61-9
ISBN-10: 1-883789-61-3

Library of Congress Cataloging-in-Publication Data:

Galusha, Diane.
  Another day, another dollar : the Civilian Conservation Corps in the Catskills / Diane Galusha. – 1st ed.
    p. cm.
  Includes bibliographical references and index.
  ISBN 978-1-883789-61-9 (trade paper)
  1. Civilian Conservation Corps (U.S.)–New York (State)–Catskill Mountains Region–History. I. Title.

  S932.N7G35 2008

  333.76'150979738–dc22

                    2008032552

The CCC patch that appears throughout this book was worn on CCC caps and was produced by Stucki Embroidery, a New Jersey company that moved to Boiceville and has operated there for decades. Courtesy of Murray Fenwick.

Cover photo: CCC enrollees planted trees by the millions in the Catskills. FDR Library.

Design: Toelke Associates

Printed in the USA

10 9 8 7 6 5 4 3 2 1

DEDICATION

This book is dedicated with affection
to Michael Strada,
whose joy and pride in the memories
of his CCC service
inspired me to write it.

Map key

Locations (approximate) of Civilian Conservation Corps camps highlighted in this book

1   Boiceville Camp P-53

2   Tannersville Camp S-97

3   Margaretville Camp S-133

4   Ten Mile River Camp S(P)-85

5   Deposit (McClure) Camp P-76

6   Masonville Camp S-100

7   Laurens (Gilbert Lake) Camp SP-11

8   Davenport Camp S-51

9   Breakabeen Camp S-93

10   Livingstonville Camp S-119

11   Gallupville Camp SCS-5

Base map prepared by Larry Kelly, edited by Ron Toelke

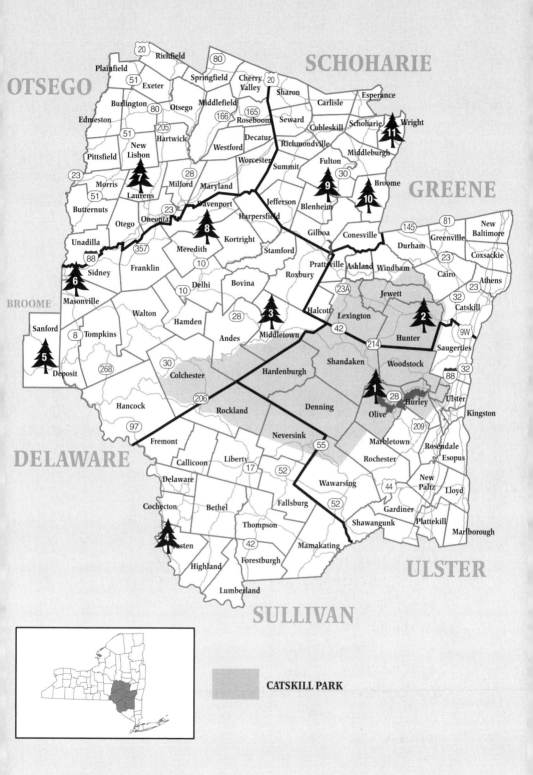

OTSEGO

SCHOHARIE

GREENE

BROOME

DELAWARE

ULSTER

SULLIVAN

20 Richfield
Plainfield
51 Exeter
Springfield
Cherry Valley
20 Sharon
Esperance
Wright
11

Burlington
80 Otsego
Middlefield
166 Roseboom
165 Carlisle
Seward
Cobleskill
Schoharie
Edmeston
205
Hartwick
Decatur
Richmondville
Middleburgh
23 Pittsfield
New Lisbon
Westford
Worcester
Summit
Fulton
9
Broome
10
Morris
28 Milford
Maryland
Jefferson
Blenheim
51 Laurens
Davenport
Harpersfield
Butternuts
23 Oneonta
8
Gilboa
Conesville
145 Greenville
New Baltimore
Otego
357
Meredith
Kortright
Stamford
Prattsville Ashland
Durham
Coxsackie
Unadilla
88
Franklin
10
Bovina
Roxbury
Windham
23 Cairo
Athens
6 Sidney
Delhi
Jewett
81
Masonville
10
Halcott
23A
Lexington
2
32 Catskill
Sanford
Walton
28
Middletown
3
42
Hunter
214
9W
8 Tompkins
Hamden
Andes
Shandaken
Woodstock
Saugerties
5 Deposit
30
Colchester
Hardenburgh
1
28
88 32
Hancock
206
Rockland
Denning
Olive
Hurley
Ulster
97
Neversink
Marbletown
209
Kingston
Fremont
55
Rochester
Rosendale
Callicoon
Liberty
52
Wawarsing
44
Esopus
Delaware
17
Fallsburg
52
New Paltz
Lloyd
Cochecton
Bethel
Gardiner
Plattekill
Marlborough
Thompson
Shawangunk
Tusten
4
42
Mamakating
Highland
Forestburgh
Lumberland

CATSKILL PARK

CONTENTS

FOREWORD

NEEDED: A GREEN CORPS

In the forested Northeast, where I live, you occasionally come across big stands of red pine. They're wonderful trees—jigsaw puzzle bark, a gorgeous hue against snow or blue sky—but if you know the history, they have another meaning, too, just as sweet. Red pine are a fairly rare native species in this area, but they were one of the trees of choice for the Civilian Conservation Corps (CCC) in the 1930s. They grow straight; they make good phone poles. For whatever set of silvicultural reasons, there are a lot of these groves of 70-year-old trees. Every time I wander through one, I think of Franklin Roosevelt and try to imagine the crews that came out to plant them.

We usually talk about New Deal programs in terms of their effect on the mood of Americans—they restored hope, they gave people back their dignity and so on. Sometimes we talk about how they helped get the economy afloat again. But there was another result: the hundreds of thousands of actual projects that were built in those years. Hiking trails, city halls, bridges, park gazebos, public plazas, dams, and on and on. For my money, that's the kind of work that needs doing now, as we face a crisis even greater than the Depression: the quick unraveling of the planet's climate system in the face of our endless emissions of carbon dioxide.

Many people have used the Apollo Project (or the Manhattan Project) as the template for how we can quickly wean ourselves off fossil fuels and replace them with renewable sources of energy. That's good as far as it goes—we do need new technologies. But in a sense our task is almost the reverse of the Apollo Project. Instead of focusing our resources to land a few people on the moon, we need to spread them out to affect everyone. It's as if we've got to get the whole nation into orbit, and fast. And for that, the Works

Progress Administration (WPA) and the CCC (and the industrial thrust to gear up for World War II) may provide a better analogy.

The people hired by these agencies went out and did things, and did them in large numbers—the CCC planted 3 billion trees (which would be no small help with global warming). Imagine an army of similar size trained to insulate American homes and stick solar photovoltaic panels on their roofs. They could achieve, within a year or two, easily noticeable effects on our energy consumption; our output of carbon dioxide might actually begin to level off. And imagine them laying trolley lines back down in our main cities or helping erect windmills across the plains. All this work would have real payoff—and none of it can be outsourced. You're not sending your house to China so they can stuff it with cellulose.

The Depression and the war that followed were the last great civilization-challenging events; global warming is the next threat on that scale. It stands to reason we'd turn for instruction to how the challenge was met last time.

Arriving on the seventy-fifth anniversary of the start of the Civilian Conservation Corps, Diane Galusha's examination of the long-forgotten contributions of the CCC in the Catskill Mountain region of New York is a compelling story that illuminates both history and a possible path into the future. Her book serves as a vivid reminder of what we owe to the people who crafted and implemented this far-reaching New Deal program aimed at reversing decades of environmental abuse. It also offers a glimpse of how, with the same sort of vision, cooperation, hard work and political will we might tackle the earth-altering changes that darken our very doorstep.

Bill McKibben, August 2008

Environmental activist, award-winning writer, and scholar in residence at Middlebury College, Bill McKibben is author of The End of Nature *and the architect of the nation-wide 2007 Stepitup campaign to initiate public action on climate change.*

Acknowledgments

I am indebted to many wonderful people without whose help this book would not have seen print.

First, I owe a debt of gratitude to 14 men who graciously shared with me their recollections, photographs and memorabilia of life in the Civilian Conservation Corps camps of this region. They are Dominick August, the late Robert Barnes, the late Doug "Red" Charles, Robert Donahue, Merlin "Dutch" DuBois, the late Hank Geary, Herb Glass, Stanton Hogan, John Jankowski, Louis Kole Sr., the late Ed Ocker, William Reich, Bill Ronovech and Michael Strada.

Family members of former CCC enrollees also provided invaluable material. Sincere thanks go to Roberta August, Lena Barnes, Socha Jean Buchanan, Ruth Dietz, Marian Egnaczak, Karen Feltman, Bob Hill, Patricia Houston, Helen Irving, Joe Monteleone and Kathy Rollison.

For memories, anecdotes and historical information that helped flesh out the story of the CCC's impact on the Catskills I am grateful to George and Matina Billias, Doug Blakelock, Frank Carl, Bud Eckert, Howard Etts Jr., Gerald Hamm, Justine Hommel, Jean Judge, Michael Kudish, Bob Reed, Lester Rosa, Bill Sanford, Orville Slutzky, Allegra Tomlinson and LeRoy Winchell.

John Dowd, Sanford Shelton and Rich Ranieri generously offered the fruits of their considerable research on the CCC.

Other individuals who provided photographs, maps, memorabilia and information included Evy Avery, Graydon Ballard, Daniel Beams, Sally Beams, Margaret Bliss, Anne Doerge, Ed Engelman, Eric Fedde, Lonnie Gale, Rose Halvorsen, John Ham, Kevin Hamilton, Paul Hartmann, Neila Hayes, Doug Helms, Carol Hendrix, Les Hendrix, Carolee Inskeep, Raphael Klein, David Malatsky, Erika Morris, Julianne Newton, Linda Norris, Ann Parsons, Marty

Podskoch, Bill Rhoads, Phil Skowfoe, Susan Smith, Cory Telarico, Roy Todd and the late Wally VanHouten.

The story of the CCC cannot be told without an understanding of forest history. Catskills experts Michael Kudish, Ed Van Put, Norman Van Valkenburgh and Ray Wood patiently answered any and all of my questions about trees and streams and mountain geography.

Gene Morris at the National Archives and Records Administration was my conduit to official inspection reports and correspondence related to the camps. The staffs at the New York State Archives and the New York State Library in Albany, the FDR Presidential Library and the Franklin D. Roosevelt National Historic Site Archives in Hyde Park, and the Library of Congress in Washington, DC, were most helpful as I sought not only CCC information, but also background on the troubled 1930s and groundbreaking New Deal programs.

The New York State Department of Environmental Conservation and the New York State Office of Parks, Recreation and Historic Preservation provided assistance in sorting out CCC projects done under their respective purviews. The Forest History Society was a source for a rarely seen photograph of Gifford Pinchot.

The small libraries and archival collections in our midst are treasure troves of local and regional history. Staff members and volunteers of the following organizations and institutions have my admiration and sincere thanks for working in near obscurity to preserve the remnants of our shared heritage: The Best House, Middleburgh; Broome County Library, Binghamton; Cannon Free Library, Delhi; Catskill Center for Conservation and Development, Arkville; Davenport Historical Society; Delaware County Historical Association, Delhi; Fairview Public Library, Margaretville; the Vedder Research Library of the Greene County Historical Society in Coxsackie; Huntington Memorial Library, Oneonta; Kingston Area Library; Middleburgh Public Library; Mountain Top Historical

Society, Haines Falls; New York State Civilian Conservation Corps Museum at Gilbert Lake State Park, Laurens; Ogden Free Library, Walton; Schoharie County Historical Society and Old Stone Fort Museum, Schoharie; Sidney Historical Society and Museum; Stamford Library; and the Tusten Historical Society at Western Sullivan Public Library's Tusten-Cochecton Branch, Narrowsburg.

I am so grateful for the careful review provided by several people with considerable knowledge on specific topical areas covered by this book. My thanks to Carol Clement, John Dowd, Carolee Inskeep, Joe Monteleone, Rich Ranieri, Ed Van Put and Norm Van Valkenburgh for reviewing chapters; to Doug Smith for helping piece together the list of CCC camps that worked on State Parks; and to Owen Lee for his assistance with the Soil Conservation Service camps list.

Special thanks go to Tom Patton, an accomplished historian and a fine writer, for reading the entire manuscript and offering corrections and suggestions for improvement. I would like to think I came close to meeting his high standards.

Additional much-appreciated editorial support was provided by Lori Anander, the late August Basani, Matina Billias, Joy Giardino, Natalie Mortensen, Christl Riedman and Ed Volmar. Ron Toelke and Barbara Kempler-Toelke did an outstanding job designing the book and its covers.

Thank you to Larry Kelly, who made the map and never complained as I asked for changes, and more changes.

Bill McKibben is one of today's foremost advocates for careful stewardship of the Earth's resources, and I am honored by his eloquent foreword and his gracious support of this book project.

Finally, to Debbie Allen and Steve Hoare of Black Dome Press, a thousand thank-yous for fitting this project into your busy publishing schedule so that it could be released in 2008 to mark the 75th anniversary of the New Deal and of the launch of the CCC.

Diane Galusha

Introduction

"Another day, another dollar;
a million days, I'll be a millionaire."

You can almost hear the cynicism and the weariness in that statement from the Civilian Conservation Corps (CCC) recruit who is believed to have first uttered it in the dark days of the Great Depression, a time when jobs were hard, if not impossible, to find, money was scarce, and the commodity in shortest supply was hope.

Yet those words contain an odd note of optimism that, with time and hard work, things might just get better. It was the CCC that ignited that spark of hope in millions of young men and began to pull the nation out of the depths of despair.

The CCC, a federal program established in 1933, put youth to work in the nation's parks and forests, and paid them $30 a month—a dollar a day. Most of that money was sent home to support families struggling mightily to keep bread on their tables.

When Franklin Delano Roosevelt took office that year as the nation's 32nd president, 12 million people, almost a quarter of the nation's workforce, were out of work. Mortgages had been foreclosed on thousands of homes and farms. Bank failures had swept away savings. Factories had shut down, cutting industrial production to the lowest level ever recorded. Mines had closed. Railroads had gone bankrupt. Men who had once been able to support their families were reduced to selling apples on street corners or traveling the countryside looking for odd jobs.

A cheerful group of Civilian Conservation Corps enrollees posed for Leonard Monteleone's camera during a work day in the Catskills. Joseph Monteleone

The situation was even worse for teenagers and young men[*] who were way down the employment pecking order. It was estimated that this army of unemployed youth numbered five million. Even when they could find work, it was only in part-time or sporadic jobs. Many who quit school at 13, 14 or 15 to try to help their families found themselves hitchhiking around the country in search of work.

FDR wasted no time in addressing this situation. On March 9, 1933, five days after assuming the presidency, he called together the secretaries of war, agriculture and the interior, the director of the budget, and others to discuss an idea to put unemployed young men aged 18 to 25 to work on forestry, flood control, soil erosion and other natural-resource conservation projects. It took only hours for this group and their staffs to draft a bill that would win passage in both the House and the Senate less than three weeks later.

[*]Young, unemployed women also felt the pangs of joblessness, but they were not allowed in the CCC. See "The She-She-She Camp."

The resulting legislation, the Emergency Conservation Work Act, created what came to be known as the Civilian Conservation Corps, the CCC, the first and arguably the most popular among a dizzying procession of acronym agencies established in the first 100 days of the Roosevelt administration's "New Deal."

On April 6, less than a month after the president called the first meeting to discuss this new initiative, the first recruit in "Roosevelt's Forest Army" was enrolled in Pennsylvania. On April 17, the first CCC camp—Camp Roosevelt—opened in the George Washington Memorial Forest in Luray, Virginia. By July 1, 1933, 1,300 camps were in operation, manned by 275,000 enrollees.

Over the next nine years, before an improving economy and World War II eliminated the need for the CCC, three and a half million young men would serve at 4,500 CCC camps in every state as well as several Indian nations, Alaska, Hawaii, Puerto Rico and the Virgin Islands.

In New York State, 210,000 enrollees at 161 camps developed many public campgrounds, built hiking, skiing and horseback riding trails, established game refuges, built dams to create swimming areas and waterfowl breeding sites, constructed five headquarters for Conservation Department Rangers, conducted stream restoration and erosion control work and helped farmers implement soil conservation measures.

They also planted more than 221 million trees and did whatever they could to protect these seedlings and the surrounding forests by eradicating insects and disease-hosting plants, erecting 19 fire lookout towers, building 392 miles of access roads and 1,207 ponds to provide water for fighting forest fires.

The Catskills benefited greatly from the work of enrollees stationed at several CCC camps in and around the region. These camps included Boiceville in Ulster County, Tannersville in Greene County, Margaretville, Davenport and Masonville in Dela-

The Kelly Hollow Trail meanders through state land reforested by the men of Margaretville CCC Company 1230.

Diane Galusha

ware County, Breakabeen, Livingstonville and Gallupville in Schoharie County, Laurens and Hartwick in Otsego County, Narrowsburg in Sullivan County, and McClure in Broome County, just over the Delaware County line.

City boys and their country cousins, under the tutelage of local woodsmen and mechanics, wielded axes, mattocks and shovels to transform the Catskills in subtle and significant ways. If you have enjoyed hiking the Kelly Hollow trail through fragrant stands of giant red pine, the view from the Mt. Utsayantha fire tower, an afternoon at the beach at North Lake, dreaming into a campfire at Woodland Valley, Beaverkill or Devil's Tombstone campsites, angling for trout in the Schoharie Creek or finding shelter from the rain in the Fox Hollow lean-to, then you have the CCC boys to thank for it.

Sadly, most of them are no longer around to accept our appreciation. This book is an attempt to pay them belated tribute and to document the legacy of the CCC in the Catskills.

Schenectady Sub-District 2 CCC Yearbook, 1936; Perry H. Merrill, *Roosevelt's Forest Army, A History of the Civilian Conservation Corps 1933–1942*; NYS Conservation Department, Annual Report to the Legislature, 1941

Chapter 1
For the Love of Trees

When the Civilian Conservation Corps—the "Forest Army"—took to the woods, its main mission was to restore, enhance and protect a resource close to the hearts of two presidents named Roosevelt: trees.

Theodore Roosevelt (Teddy, or TR) , who called his program of reform and conservation a "Square Deal" for America, and his fifth cousin, Franklin Delano Roosevelt (FDR), proponent of his own "New Deal," were ardent outdoorsmen and nature lovers. Both had served as New York State governor, and both had worked to conserve the forests of the state and the nation. Both men also recognized the revenue to be derived from tourists, timber and other forest use.

During his tenure as governor in the years 1899 and 1900, Teddy Roosevelt signed the 1900 Davis Palisades Act, which created the Palisades Interstate Park spanning New York and New Jersey, and signed legislation extending the State Forest Preserve in Delaware, Greene, Sullivan and Ulster Counties. In his 1900 Address to the Legislature, he urged that the Adirondacks and Catskills "should be great parks kept in perpetuity for the benefit and enjoyment of our people." (The Adirondack Park had been established in 1892; the Catskill Park was designated in 1904. Both parks are made up of state-owned Forest Preserve lands, as well as private lands.)

While Teddy Roosevelt was in the White House from 1901 to 1908, approximately 230,000,000 acres of the United States were placed under public protection in the form of 5 new National Parks, 51 Wildlife Refuges, 16 National Monuments, extensive National Forests and other reserves.

In 1905 TR gave Gifford Pinchot, a college-trained forester, responsibility for administering this new wilderness domain as head of the newly organized U.S. Forest Service. Pinchot, arguing that natural resources of the West required scientific management to prevent their destruction by private developers, basically "invented" the idea of conservation, which became an accepted national goal.

A generation later, Pinchot, now governor of Pennsylvania, provided the new Roosevelt in the White House, FDR, with statis-

FDR enjoyed driving his specially equipped car through the professionally managed forest at Springwood, the family estate in Hyde Park, New York. FDR Library

tics showing the depletion of timber resources on privately held lands. He urged "large scale public acquisition of private forest lands" to check such devastation, along with a program to reforest 50 million acres of abandoned farmlands using the labor of unemployed men receiving government relief.[1]

An abandoned Schoharie County farmhouse offered mute testimony of the migration of rural families off their farms in the early decades of the twentieth century. New York State acquired thousands of abandoned farms and put crews of jobless men to work reforesting them, as shown here on State Reforestation Area #2 (at right) near Manorkill, Schoharie County. NYS Archives

FDR didn't need to be convinced of the value of forests to the nation's purse, and its psyche. Raised at Springwood, the family's forested estate in Hyde Park, New York, he had spent his youth exploring the old-growth forest, hills and streams on the property overlooking the Hudson River. In 1910 he was elected to the New York State Senate, where he was appointed

chairman of the Senate Committee on Forestry. In 1911 he hired a forester to develop a management plan for Springwood's fields and forests and the following year he ordered a few thousand seedlings, from the state's premiere tree nursery at Saratoga, to be planted in selected plots. Over the next four decades, FDR oversaw the planting of 550,000 replacement and plantation trees on his 1,000+ acres.[2]

He also established a vigorous Christmas tree plantation, selling thousands every year to wholesalers who bought them for from 50¢ to $3 each on the stump.[3] While in the White House, he requested his staff at Hyde Park to ship special trees to special people. In 1943 the Crown Princess of Norway and British Prime Minister Winston Churchill received Springwood greenery.[4]

FDR's interest in forestry was not simply a parochial one. Like many New Yorkers of his age, he had seen the lingering effects of the destructive tanning and wood acid industries that had cleared entire mountainsides and practically eliminated the

hemlock tree in New York. He watched with dismay the decimation of the state's woodlands by uncontrolled logging to meet the demands for housing, furnishings, railroad ties and fuel. Forest fires took a terrible toll, and rivers often ran brown from soil washed off barren hillsides.

In 1885 the New York State Legislature created the Adirondack and Catskill Forest Preserves to protect some of the most vulnerable areas from further destruction. On Arbor Day, 1901, the first reforestation project in the state took place in the Catskills, where spruce and pine seedlings from Cornell were set out in a denuded patch of the north slope of Wittenberg Mountain in Ulster County. The following year, the first large-scale state nursery was established at Brown's Station in the Town of Olive, Ulster County. That nursery was discontinued in 1906 (it is now submerged beneath New York City's Ashokan Reservoir, completed in 1915), but ten

New Yorkers had a love affair with trees in the 1910s and 1920s, flocking to forestry field days like this one at Pine Grove Farm, Walton, on August 14, 1924, when 400,000 tree seedlings were sold for replanting. NYS Archives

The State Conservation Department promoted reforestation by taking exhibits like this one, in 1933, on the road. NYS Archives

more were eventually sited around the state to supply the growing need for reforestation stock.[5]

Over the years, legislation and bond issues enabled the state to purchase thousands of acres to add to the Preserves ("forever wild" land within the Catskill and Adirondack Parks) and to create new State Forest tracts elsewhere. Much of that land was abandoned farmland whose owners had headed west for greener pastures, moved to the cities for greater opportunities, or lost their hardscrabble lands to bank foreclosure or taxes. During the closing years of the 1920s, an estimated 600,000 people per year fled their farms across the nation.[6]

"The State did buy at a low price, $10 an acre or maybe a little less than that, but it was high land. It wasn't profitable to farm it, and wasn't good for pastureland. It was more profitable for people to sell to the state than keep it and pay taxes on it," said Edward West of Jewett, Greene County, in a 1984 interview. "They could use those few dollars to buy a piece of machinery to maybe farm lower land." West worked with the Conservation Department from 1919 to 1967, spending much of that time surveying Preserve boundaries. But in 1927 and 1928, he says, "I planted a million trees on Forest Preserve land. Of course, I had a big crew."

Frank Dann posed in the 1930s with nine-year-old trees at Northfield in Walton. Like many landowners of his generation, Dann was an avid forester. Carolee Inskeep

A number of public and private initiatives in the 1920s encouraged reforestation. The Free Tree Bill of 1920 made seedlings available to municipalities and school districts for planting on government lands in an effort to stabilize stream banks and curb erosion. The State Conservation Commission (it became the Conservation Department in 1926) gave thousands of seedlings for demonstration projects to prove the value of converting "waste land" to productive timber stands. Reporting on April 23, 1926, that more than 200,000 Norway spruce and Scotch pine would be planted on 200 acres of state land that had been the Ward and Kelly farms in the Millbrook Valley near Margaretville, the *Catskill Mountain News* suggested that farmers under the age of 30 might want to do the same: "Here is something that will be as good or better than an insurance policy due at the age of 60 or 62."

County Farm Bureau Forestry Committees held tours and educational field days at local tree farms where landowners could learn what species of trees to plant, how to keep them alive and how to manage their forests for wildlife and revenue. One such field day was held in August 1924 at Pine Grove Farm near Walton where, in 1914, Charles DuMond began a lifelong effort to reforest the 350-acre farm adjacent to Forest Hall, another reforestation site he developed with his brother-in-law, Frank Dann. Thousands of people attended the 1924 event. According to the Walton Reporter, 400,000 tree seedlings were sold at the field day by State Forest Superintendent Clifford Pettis at a cost of $2 per thousand.

The state also gave seedlings to 4-H members. Delaware County youths each received 1,000 in 1933, enough to cover 40 acres.

The tanning, wood chemical and logging industries wreaked havoc on the Catskills during the nineteenth and early twentieth centuries. This undated photo shows tree tops and limbs left atop Hunter Mountain. NYS Archives

Twenty-six 4-H clubs in Greene County got 26,000 trees in 1934. Orville Slutzky of Hunter recalled planting them with his 4-H club during Easter vacation one year.[7]

The state encouraged schools to plant forests as a way to reduce the burden on taxpayers, and dozens of schools participated. In Walton the school board voted in September 1924 to appropriate $300 to purchase land to start a school forest. School administrators anticipated that 1,000 board feet of white pine harvested from 60 to 80 acres each year could yield $900 to $1,200 a year.[8] Of course, they'd have to wait 40 years for the trees to reach harvestable size, but that didn't deter them. A large and enthusiastic forestry club was formed, and students planted 122,500 tree seedlings between 1927 and 1934 to create the largest school forest in New York State.[9]

An early attempt at reforestation in the Catskills is shown in this photo of men carrying seedlings for planting on Timothyberg Mountain, adjoining Mt. Tremper in Shandaken, circa 1901. NYS Archives

In April 1921, students from the Raymond Riordan School in Highland, anxious to plant a living tribute to their Hudson Valley neighbor, famed naturalist John Burroughs who had died the previous month, journeyed, seedlings in hand, to Fleischmanns. There they asked District Forest Ranger Stratton Todd where there might be some vacant state land to establish a memorial forest. He directed them to an open plot on a former farm on Rose Mountain in the Town of Shandaken, where they planted 14,000 trees and erected a concrete monument that still stands.[10]

As governor of New York from 1928 to 1932, FDR was concerned about the plight of struggling farmers. He made it a priority to seek legislation and policies that would increase farmers' earning capacity. He saw farmers working inferior soils on marginal lands and reaping poor harvests of crops, grain and fruit, and he thought they would be better off selling this substandard land to the state, which would then reforest it and transform it into state parks and woodlands for the benefit of residents and visitors.

Governor Roosevelt and Conservation Commissioner Henry Morgenthau Jr. (later secretary of the treasury under President Roosevelt) garnered widespread legislative and public support for the idea as they argued the ecological, social and fiscal benefits of statewide reforestation. The adoption of the State Reforestation Law of 1929 and the approval by voters of the 1931 Hewitt Amendment to the State Constitution, along with a $19 million bond issue, made the idea a reality.[11]

The acts authorized the Conservation Department to acquire, by gift or purchase, "Reforestation Areas" of at least 500 acres of contiguous land to be forever dedicated to maintenance of forests for "watershed protection, production of timber and for recreation and kindred purposes." These areas became the nucleus of the present-day New York State Forest system and were the focus of many of the Civilian Conservation Corps' labors in the 1930s.

A Passion for Forests

"A people without children would face a hopeless future; a country without trees is almost as helpless." Teddy Roosevelt's plea for his countrymen's help in planting trees topped John D. Clarke's Christmas card one year, for Clarke was a man on a mission.

A onetime mining executive, an attorney and a U.S. congressman, Clarke (1873–1933) was a forester at heart. A native of Hobart, Delaware County, he found his life's purpose at Arbor Hill, a Delhi estate founded by Revolutionary War veteran Ebenezer Foote. Clarke acquired the estate in 1915 and planted row upon row of evergreens there.

Clarke represented the 34th District of New York from 1921 to 1925, and again from 1927 to 1933. In 1924 he coauthored legislation that propelled reforestation on private lands and forest acquisition by the federal government.

The Clarke-McNary Act directed the secretary of agriculture, in cooperation with the states and with land-grant colleges, to aid farmers by educating them about establishing, renewing, managing—and benefiting from—woodlots, windbreaks and shelterbelts. It also enabled the secretary of agriculture to accept donated lands to be added to National Forests and to search out lands with valuable water and timber resources for potential addition to those forests.

Locally, Clarke loaned 10 acres of his property for use as a 4-H summer camp in 1927, and the following year he leased the property to the camp for the annual "rent" of 100 newly planted trees on the land. The camp was named Shankitunk, said to be an Indian word for "woody place." Today it includes a "model forest," developed by the New York City Department of Environmental Protection, the Watershed Agricultural Council and other partners, where forest management techniques are demonstrated.

Clifford R. Pettis is another Delaware County native who gained prominence in the forestry field.

John D. Clarke brought his interest in trees to Washington where, as a congressman from Delaware County, he co-authored legislation that encouraged federal acquisition of lands for reforestation. Delaware County Historical Association

Clifford Pettis, a DeLancey native, was New York's Superintendent of Forests from 1910 to 1927. He developed the tree nursery program and was called the "Father of Reforestation." NYS Archives

Born in DeLancey in 1877 the son of a farmer and grandson of a logger, Pettis attended Delaware Academy but graduated from Ithaca High School in 1896. A member of the first class of the Cornell College of Forestry in 1901, he went to work for the state's Forest, Fish & Game Commission and is credited with developing a system for nursery development and management that was adopted by the U.S. Department of Agriculture.

Pettis became Superintendent of State Forests in the Conservation Commission in 1911, a post he held through 1927, the year he died. Hailed as "The Father of Reforestation," he was buried at Paul Smiths, New York. A 3,000-acre plot planted in 1906–1909 between Ray Brook and Lake Placid was named the Pettis Memorial Forest in 1929.

Biographical Directory of the US Congress 1774–Present; "76 Years of Fun-tastic Camp!" (4-H Camp Shankitunk history, 2004); Clarke family Christmas card (undated), The Clarke-McNary Act of June 7, 1924; *Cornell Alumni News,* April 19, 1923; NYS Archives, Conservation Department photograph collection, Clifford Pettis image 14297-87 SARA No. 1639

Clifford Pettis developed Saratoga Nursery into the principal tree seedling supplier for reforestation efforts in New York State.
NYS Archives

FDR's victory for conservation in his home state would soon be replicated on the national stage. People across the country were beginning to see the beneficial possibilities.

"There is one thing about Governor Roosevelt of New York that we heartily approve," read an editorial in a rural newspaper in far-off Iowa. "That is the advocacy of reforestation, the planting of trees in the waste places of New York, and it might well be extended to all other states."[12]

CHAPTER 2
GONE WITH THE WIND:
THE
GREAT DEPRESSION

Although Margaret Mitchell's best-selling and Pulitzer Prize-winning novel of the Civil War was not published until 1935, its title aptly describes the evaporation of money, jobs and optimism precipitated years earlier by the stock market crash of 1929.

To be sure, the Depression did not descend overnight on unsuspecting Americans. During the so-called "Roaring Twenties," economic forces had been building toward this calamity: rapid industrialization produced more goods than the nation could consume, corporate mergers yielded monopolies in critical areas of the economy, the farm sector stagnated as elected leaders insisted "the business of government is business," and rabid stock market speculation by investors large and small provided tinder for the eruption that would consume American society.

The erosion in buying power was felt from top to bottom on the economic food chain. Manufacturing output plummeted as industries reduced inventories and laid off workers. Thousands of small businesses closed. Farm income dropped by half over the next three years while farm debt rose by a proportional amount, forcing thousands of families off the land and into the cities where they joined the throngs of the unemployed. The jobless numbered 4.3 million in 1930, 8 million in 1931, 12 million in 1932. Average annual family income slid from $2,300 in 1929 to $1,600 or less in 1932.[1]

People wait in a breadline to be fed in New York City. In the absence of substantial gov-ernment relief programs during 1932, free food was distributed to the needy with private funds in some urban centers. FDR Library

An army of out-of-work people roamed the nation's highways and railroads looking for jobs. Former white-collar workers clustered at construction sites or any place rumored to be hiring. Shantytowns of the homeless and dispossessed were everywhere. They called them "Hoovervilles" for the president they blamed for their predicament. Soup kitchens kept many from starving.

President Roosevelt issued his famous call to action to combat the Depression during his first inaugural address on March 4, 1933. FDR Library

President Herbert Hoover, insisting that the economic down-turn was "just a passing incident in our national life," believed in the laissez-faire approach: that the underlying strength of the capi-talist system would turn things around and the good old days would make a comeback. Neither he nor his advisors believed that gov-ernment should directly assist homeless, jobless and hungry people with cash payments. To the Hoover administration the "dole" (a form of unemployment relief adopted by the British) smacked of socialism and threatened to make its recipients lazy and dependent. Rather, it should be left to churches, community chests and other local aid networks to provide rescue and relief for the desperate.[2]

By contrast, in New York, Governor Franklin Roosevelt, recogniz-ing that private agencies could not cope with the magnitude of the problem, called a special session of the State Legislature in 1931 to implement a work relief program called the Temporary Emergency Relief Administration (TERA). With an initial appropriation of $20 million (raised by a 50 percent, one-year hike in the state income tax), New York became the first state to create a comprehensive, multimillion-dollar relief program to assist New York's unemployed, whose numbers grew from 656,000 in 1929 to 2,060,000 in 1933.[3]

TERA provided funds to local welfare districts, which provided home and work relief, gave free milk and lunches to schools, sup-plied equipment for subsistence gardens, and sponsored budget-ing and parenting classes. These programs assisted an estimated five million people, 40 percent of the state's population. TERA continued to operate through 1937.[4*]

FDR had appointed Isadore Strauss, president of R. H. Macy Department Store, to chair the new agency, and Strauss had

*After 1933, most of the money spent by TERA came from federal relief programs, but during this period, the new state administration of Gov. Herbert Lehman embraced the notion of government's responsibility for public welfare. It established programs for unem-ployment relief and work assistance, aid to the elderly and disabled, and public housing development. New state legislation in the 1930s also provided for collective bargaining, farm price supports and a minimum wage.

named Harry Hopkins as its executive director. Hopkins, then unknown to Roosevelt, impressed the governor with his efficient administration of TERA's initial $20 million budget. When Strauss resigned as head of TERA, Hopkins, who had earlier served as executive secretary of the New York City Bureau of Child Welfare and later as a director of the Red Cross, was promoted to replace him.

FDR's focus midway through his second term as governor shifted to a run for the presidency. On July 2, 1932, he was nominated as the Democratic Party's candidate to oppose incumbent Herbert Hoover. His acceptance speech at the Chicago Democratic Convention coined the phrase that would characterize the momentous period of change just ahead:

"I pledge myself to a new deal for the American people. Let us all here assembled constitute ourselves prophets of a new order of competence and of courage. This is more than a political campaign; it is a call to arms. Give me your help, not to win votes alone, but to win in this crusade to restore America to its own people."

FDR's platform included the radical notions of federal expenditures for relief, a large public works program, and old-age and unemployment insurance. The Democrats were also firmly in favor of ending prohibition by repealing the 18th Amendment of 1919 that banned the manufacture, transportation and sale of alcoholic beverages. (The 21st Amendment repealed the unpopular act in 1933.) Whether it was those arguments or the charisma and confidence exuded by the candidate, FDR won the Oval Office from Republican Hoover in a landslide, 22 million to 17 million popular votes, capturing the electoral votes of all but six states.[5]

After assuming the presidency in 1933, Roosevelt brought New York State's TERA Director Harry Hopkins to Washington where he joined FDR's advisors and became one of the chief architects

Hunter-Tannersville Central School was among Catskill Mountain schools constructed by men employed under the Works Progress Administration (WPA). This was one of dozens of acronym agencies established during the Depression. D. Allen

of the new president's promised New Deal. Frances Perkins, who had served as state labor commissioner under Governor Roosevelt, became labor secretary in the new administration, the first female cabinet member. In her book *The Roosevelt I Knew*, she described the New Deal as "basically an attitude that found voice in expressions like 'the people are what matter to government,' and 'a government should aim to give all the people under its jurisdiction the best possible life.'"

Toward that end, FDR's so-called "brain trust" assembled in the next two years the following work relief programs:[6]

• **The Federal Emergency Relief Administration** provided matching grants to states, which were required to set up county FERA offices where those in need applied for vouchers to be redeemed for coal, food or rent.

- **The Civil Works Administration** put men who qualified for FERA to work repairing schools, laying sewer pipes, and building roads, playgrounds and flood control facilities. A women's division employed females in nursing, cooking, furniture repair, park beautification, secretarial work and other tasks. Designed as a temporary program at the height of the emergency, the CWA was discontinued in 1934.

- **The Public Works Administration** in six years financed 34,508 public works projects such as schools, sidewalks, courthouses, post offices, hospitals and municipal water projects. More than $6 billion was spent on projects that employed half a million workers. These jobs were primarily for adults who were not necessarily on relief. Many Catskill region schools and public buildings were constructed under this program, and under the WPA.

- **The Works Progress Administration,** established during Roosevelt's second term and the so-called Second New Deal, built thousands of public facilities, highways, bridges and airports. More than eight million people were employed at an average monthly salary of $41.57. A division of the WPA included the Federal Art, Music, Theater and Writers Projects, which paid artists, musicians, actors, researchers and writers to create murals and sculpture for public buildings, and concerts and plays for communities across the land. Among its many other works was a series of guides to each of the 48 states.

- **The National Youth Administration**, another Second New Deal program, helped an estimated two million young people by giving them jobs in their high schools at $6 a month, and in colleges at $15 a month, as well as in the community. Vocational training, and cultural and educational enrichment programs were also offered. Some youths were trained in first aid to assist as emergency responders on WPA job sites. They were employed as "supplementary earners," earning one-third the pay of regular workers.

But the very first of FDR's groundbreaking lineup of "alphabet agencies"* was the one closest to his heart: the Civilian Conservation Corps.

On the Road

A pair of newspaper articles gives a hint of the impact of the wandering jobless on local communities in the early 1930s:

An Indication of Present Times

It is a sad commentary on current times that so many unfortunates who travel the road seeking either employment or even food are obliged to seek help for a night in the village lockup. ... It is a humane provision of the law that these applicants shall be provided with over night shelter. Three years ago requests for night shelter were rare, but conditions have now changed. Chief of Police W. R. Dickinson says that the average applications during the winter was from 8 to 9 per night, and the total from January 1st to May 15th is 494 given shelter. The applicants are in most cases perfectly orderly and leave in early morning. If any request breakfast Chief Dickinson is authorized to give a 35 cent ticket on the Star lunch.

Unnamed Sidney, New York, newspaper
May 19, 1932

"Tourist" Problem of Three Towns

Jefferson has a novel way of handling these "tourists." When a request is made for supper or shelter for the night ... the Welfare Commissioner writes an order for groceries not to exceed thirty cents. This order the visitor takes to the grocery (there is only one in Jefferson) and

*For a list of New Deal agencies, see Appendix A.

the grocer permits his customer to choose what he likes ... a loaf of bread, a small piece of butter, a bit of coffee, a bit of sugar, possibly a small can of beans. The next objective is the lodging place, a small but comfortable one-room building in which is a double bed, a bunk fashioned from a porch swing, blankets, a few utensils and dishes, and a flat topped stove. Wood and kindling is provided by the village. Water is had at the garage next door. [The tourist] washes his shirt and socks and hangs them up to dry. Then he shaves. The next morning he prepares breakfast. Then he departs for the next town, for he must forever be on the move or risk arrest.

Stamford Mirror-Recorder
February 16, 1933

Hitchhikers looking for work or a place to stay were a common sight during the lean days of the Depression. FDR Library

CHAPTER 3
THE
FOREST
ARMY

By the time FDR took office in March 1933, the idea of a conservation-based work relief program had been percolating in his head for a while.

He had supported its implementation as governor of New York, where state parks, and the unemployed, benefited from the Reforestation Act of 1929. His 1932 speech accepting his party's nomination as president included the outline of a plan to employ a million men to confront "a future of soil erosion and timber famine."[1] He took note of various conservation work relief models in countries like Bulgaria, the Netherlands, Germany and Canada, where single, homeless, unemployed men were put to work in provincial and national parks.

And as president-elect, he sought out facts, figures and advice to support his ideas.

In a letter to Roosevelt dated January 20, 1933, former Chief U.S. Forester Gifford Pinchot claimed that, of 271 million acres of forestlands owned by commercial interests, 55 million had been "virtually devastated" by improper forestry practices. He recommended that the government take over millions of acres of tax-delinquent forest and abandoned farmlands, and utilize the unemployed for work including "planting, thinning, release cuttings, the removal of highly inflammable snags and windfalls, a large scale attack on serious insect epidemics, the control of ero-

sion, the construction of roads, trails and telephone lines, and the development of camp sites
and other recreational facilities.

"There is no single domestic step that can be
taken that will mean so much to the future of the
United States as this one," concluded Pinchot.
"In proportion to the benefits, the cost would
be almost trivial. Indeed, it is hard to see where
opposition could come from."[2]

But reaction to this concept was not univer-
sally positive. The *Delaware Express*, for example,
sneered at the idea in commentary published in
the Delhi paper July 8, 1932, following FDR's first
public mention of the proposal in his nomination

*Former Chief U.S. Forester
Gifford Pinchot provided
FDR with statistics sup-
porting the president's
proposal to establish a
program to "confront a
future of soil erosion and
timber famine." Pinchot
is at left in this photo,
taken while he was com-
missioner of the Pennsyl-
vania Dept. of Forestry.
He is shown viewing a
working erosion model at
the Pennsylvania Forestry
Association Convention
in Pittsburgh in June
1921.* Forest History Society,
Durham, North Carolina

acceptance speech. "The Hyde Park Messiah would have 10,000,000 unemployed get right to work planting trees. To be sure, only 1,000,000 would do the manual labor, but that would keep the other 9,000,000 occupied in supervisory capacities. Whatever else may be in store for future generations, they will have plenty of shade."

The president, with Agriculture Secretary Henry Wallace and Civilian Conservation Corps Director Robert Fechner, surrounded by CCC enrollees at Shenandoah, Virginia, August 12, 1933. FDR Library

As details of the plan were formalized, opponents objected that the program would take jobs from people currently working in the forest industry, and that the dollar-a-day pay rate would depress wages across the board and enhance class divisions. But with the country in a desperate way,

The "Moral Equivalent of War"

Some say it was Harvard philosopher William James's essay, "The Moral Equivalent of War," that influenced FDR to pursue the notion of putting men to work in the nation's forests.

While Roosevelt claimed to have developed the idea on his own, his papers at the Presidential Library in Hyde Park contain a typescript excerpt of James's 1906 address, which was delivered at Stanford University and published in 1912, so it is safe to assume FDR was at least familiar with, and perhaps sympathetic with, its central theme.

In the essay, pacifist James decried the brutality and senseless destruction of war, but acknowledged that discipline, hardiness and a sense of common purpose bred by military service are essential to a productive and healthy society.

He proposed that those qualities could be instilled through another type of service, and that military conscription be replaced by "a conscription of the whole youthful population to form for a certain number of years a part of the army enlisted against *Nature*." Such work by young men would serve "to get the childishness knocked out of them ... [they would] come back into society with healthier sympathies and soberer ideas. [T]hey would tread the earth more proudly, the women would value them more highly, they would be better fathers and teachers of the following generation.

"Such a conscription, with the state of public opinion that would have required it, and the many moral fruits it would bear, would preserve in the midst of a pacific civilization the manly virtues which the military party is so afraid of seeing disappear in peace. We should get toughness without callousness, authority with as little criminal cruelty as possible, and painful work done cheerily because the duty is temporary, and threatens not, as now, to degrade the whole remainder of one's life.

"So far, war has been the only force that can discipline a whole community, and until an equivalent discipline is organized, I believe that war must have its way. But I have no serious doubt that the ordinary prides and shames of social man, once developed to a certain intensity, are capable of organizing such a moral equivalent as I have sketched, or some other just as effective for preserving manliness of type. It is but a question of time, of skillful propagandism, and of opinion-making men seizing historic opportunities."

Indeed, almost three decades later FDR seized the day by proposing in his inaugural address on March 21, 1933, "a civilian conservation corps to be used in simple work not interfering with normal employment, and confining itself to forestry, the prevention of soil erosion, flood control and similar projects."

Using verbiage and imagery similar to James's, Roosevelt stated:

"More important, however, than the material gains will be the moral and spiritual value of such work. The overwhelming majority of unemployed Americans, who are now walking the streets and receiving private or public relief, would infinitely prefer to work. We can take a vast army of these unemployed out into healthful surroundings. We can eliminate to some extent at least the threat that enforced idleness brings to spiritual and moral stability. It is not a panacea for all the unemployment but it is an essential step in this emergency."

---

and no better ideas coming from Congress, lawmakers adopted on March 31, 1933, the Emergency Conservation Work Act to employ, house, transport and equip out-of-work citizens to restore depleted natural resources.

In an executive order issued five days later, FDR named Robert Fechner to direct the effort, with the secretaries of war, agriculture, interior and labor, or their representatives, to serve on an advisory council. Ten million dollars left over from an appropriation for a Hoover-era act "to relieve destitution" was made available to Fechner for the Civilian Conservation Corps.

Many CCC enrollees were barely more than boys when they signed up for the program that fed them, clothed them, and paid them $30 a month, $25 of which went home to help their struggling families. Stanton Hogan

In a matter of weeks, the CCC was born. Here's how it worked:

The application process was set up by the Department of Labor, which worked with state and county relief commissions to establish quotas for each six-month enrollment period. Unmarried, unemployed males aged 18 to 25 were eligible to apply. Preference was given to those whose families were on relief, and $25 of the $30 monthly pay was sent home to their families. More than $662 million was thus funneled to needy families nationwide during the nine years the CCC operated.[3]

Enrollees could keep $5 per month, which they spent on toiletries, recreation or whatever they wished. They were given personal hygiene items, work clothes, uniforms, shoes and boots, coats, raingear, underwear and three square meals a day. Thirteen percent of each CCC company's men were named to assistant or administrative positions by camp supervisors and were paid a bit more per month.[4]

The "She-She-She Camp"

The act that created what came to be known as the Civilian Conservation Corps included the stipulation that "no discrimination shall be made on account of race, color or creed." It said nothing about gender, and so, while a few women were assigned indoor jobs at CCC camps and were paid "allowances" of 50¢ a week (compared to the $1 a day young men were paid), the CCC was, for all intents and purposes, a male world.

Eleanor Roosevelt felt strongly that something should be done to help the four million unemployed females, whose number included a growing proportion of homeless women and girls. Many of them had held jobs but lost them when the Depression struck, as most available employment was given to men. Married women, including teachers, hospital employees and government workers, were routinely dismissed to give employment to male "breadwinners."

To assist vulnerable single women without support, Eleanor Roosevelt lobbied for inclusion of females in the CCC, but the type of manual labor envisioned for the Corps was not deemed suitable for females. Still, she persisted, and the president agreed to find funding for women's camps if enough women were interested.

With Labor Secretary Frances Perkins, the first female cabinet member in history, Eleanor helped set up Camp Tera on Lake Tiorati in New York's Bear Mountain State Park in June of 1933. The camp was administered by TERA—the state's Temporary Employment Relief Administration, which had been set up by FDR when he was governor of New York in 1931. TERA was reimbursed for camp expenditures by the Federal Emergency Relief Administration (FERA) and by the Welfare Council of New York City, which selected the participants.

Camp Tera, though dubbed the "She-She-She Camp," was not comparable to the male CCC camps: women were not paid; they stayed only limited periods of time, and they did modest domestic projects, such as sewing. Still, it provided a safe haven for homeless or at-risk women, and it provided a model for a broader national program spurred by Eleanor Roosevelt's White House Conference on Camps for Unemployed Women, held April 30, 1934.

The conference led to the establishment by FERA of 28 experimental schools and camps for jobless females. Responsibility for the camps was turned over to the National Youth Administration (NYA), which renamed Camp Tera as Camp Jane Addams.

Ultimately, 90 such camps would be run by the NYA before they were eliminated in 1937 as part of a major cutback in New Deal programs. The camps served an estimated 8,500 women, a fraction of the 3,500,000 men employed by the CCC.

Regulating the Lives of Women: Social Welfare Policy from Colonial Times (Mimi Abramovitz); *Eleanor Roosevelt Encyclopedia* (Beasley, et al); "What of Her: Eleanor Roosevelt and Camp Tera," *New York History,* Spring 2006 (Thomas Patton)

Eleanor Roosevelt addressed a crowd during a 1933 visit to Camp Tera, which she helped establish for unemployed women near Bear Mountain in New York State. FDR Library

CCC companies were roused every morning by buglers playing reveille.
National Archives and Records Administration

If they passed the physical (which included a requirement that they have at least three masticating teeth), they were sent to a conditioning camp at a military base in their region. After a couple of weeks there, they were assigned to a company, which was assigned to a camp.

The companies and camps were run by the Army. Regular and Reserve Army officers, many of them veterans of World War I, had charge of the enrollees while they were at camp. Although there was military hierarchy and a regimented flavor to days in camp, which began with morning reveille, enrollees were assured at the outset that they had not been "drafted" and that service was both voluntary and a privilege.*

In the field the men were supervised by the agency that organized the work projects. In New York State that included agents from the State Conservation Department, Soil Conservation Service of the U.S. Department of Agriculture, and the U.S. Department of the Interior. Projects were undertaken in State Parks, on State Forest lands, and on private lands where fire protection, eradication of forest diseases and insects, and flood control was in

---

*"When an applicant enrolls, he does not enlist to become a soldier," CCC Director Fechner said in a May 6, 1933 speech. "There is no militarism in the usual sense of the word. There will be no drills, no Army salutes, no guns." Skeptics, however, remained nervous at the prospect of the Army having control of "plastically minded young men," as Lodge #459, International Association of Machinists, phrased it in a resolution expressing its disfavor. The group demanded the resignation of Fechner, a former machinist, who happened to be the union's vice-president. Fechner remained CCC chief, and union VP, until his death in 1940.

Administrators insist-ed the CCC was not the army (participants were called "enrollees" not "recruits"), but camps were run with a certain military regimentation by regu-lar and reserve army officers, like these in Margaretville. Joseph Monteleone

the general public interest and benefited the region, rather than individual property owners.[5]

Companies of about 200 men were often moved from camp to camp around the country, and their makeup changed as enrollees came and went. In the early days of the program, many men from the East were sent west by train to work in the National Parks and Forests which made up about half of the 1,437 forest work camps selected by July of 1933. Those companies often rotated back to eastern camps.

The United States was divided into nine Army Corps Areas. The Second Corps was made up of New York, New Jersey and Delaware. Of the initial 42 camps in the Second Corps, New York hosted 32, most of them in the Adirondacks.[6]

Camps were little villages, usually with five 40-man barracks buildings, a mess hall, tool house, a garage for a dozen or so trucks and tractors, water and sewage facilities, streets and sidewalks, a recreation hall, a camp store, and an education building where enrollees could take classes in everything from photography to plumbing to prepare them for life after the CCC. Many camps put out their own mimeographed newsletters.

Camps for Veterans

One of the most shameful episodes in American history led to the addition of CCC camps for veterans.

In the summer of 1932, some 15,000 down-and-out veterans of World War I descended on Washington, D.C. They were there to demand their so-called "bonus" payment—$1 a day for WWI service in the United States, $1.25 a day for service abroad—that had been pledged by 1924 legislation for payout in 1945. The vets, many of them destitute and unable to support their families, wanted the money now.

Led by Walter Waters, an Oregon veteran who summoned them to action, veterans from across the country, many with families, made their way by box car, truck and on foot to the nation's capital, where they constituted the largest mass demonstration in Washington up to that time. Encamped in 27 tent cities and squatting in abandoned buildings, the "Bonus Expeditionary Force" (BEF) occupied Washington for several weeks. When a bill authorizing immediate cash payout of the bonus was approved by the House of Representatives but failed in the Senate, the assembled veterans lingered in D.C., with no place to go and no money to get there. A special bill providing $100,000 to transport the veterans out of the District was signed by President Herbert Hoover on July 9, and vets were given a deadline of July 24 to leave town.

With thousands remaining after the deadline, D.C. police began evicting squatters from downtown buildings. When conflict erupted, Hoover, on July 28, ordered the Army, under the command of General Douglas MacArthur, to quell the disorder and clear the streets. Troops on horseback and on foot, bearing sabers and bayonets and backed by tanks, marched through Washington's streets attacking demonstrators and firing tear gas canisters. They torched the largest of the encampments, burning hundreds of tents and shacks to the ground along with the marchers' personal belongings. Two veterans and a baby died; many people, including women and children, were injured.

Ephraim Counser, photographed at a New York State CCC camp in November of 1933, bore the imprint of experience as did many World War I-era veterans who served in CCC veteran companies.
FDR Library

Despite this traumatic conclusion to the 1932 march, the BEF returned to D.C. in 1933 and was allowed to set up camp at the Army's Fort Hunt near Mt. Vernon in Alexandria, Virginia. Though there was a new president, the result was the same: no immediate payout of the veterans' bonus. FDR instead issued an executive order on May 11 allowing veterans of previous conflicts (WWI, Spanish-American War, Philippines Insurrection, Morocco Expedition and the Boxer Rebellion) to join the Civilian Conservation Corps. About 2,500 of them accepted the offer. In a May 23 memo to the president, Press Secretary Stephen Early enumerated the numbers of veterans leaving for CCC conditioning camps, concluding, "The bonus camp at Fort Hunt is being struck tonight, and all is peaceful on the Potomac."

Vets joining the CCC were paid the same dollar a day as the junior enrollees, with three-quarters of their monthly allowance going to dependents or, if they had no dependents, into an account to be held until they left the CCC. They could stay as long as they liked and would be housed, wherever possible, in camps separate from younger corpsmen.

Twenty-six CCC camps in New York State were designated veteran camps. Camp S-119 in Livingstonville, Schoharie County, which was

Camp S-119 in Livingstonville, Schoharie County, housed several CCC companies made up of veterans. Today some of its buildings serve as residences. Diane Galusha

established in August of 1935, housed Veteran Companies 2203, 397, and 2234 in its six years of existence. (A junior company, #1246, was stationed there during 1936.)

Many WWI veterans did not join the CCC and again traveled to Washington in 1934 seeking their bonus. Instead, they were given passage to "Veterans' Rehabilitation Camps" where they were employed under the Federal Emergency Relief Administration (FERA). Many were shipped to FERA work camps in the south. On Labor Day of 1935, a deadly hurricane blew across the Florida Keys where 600 veterans were working to build a road linking the Upper Keys to Key West. More than 250 veterans died in the storm. Among those sent to locate and retrieve their bodies were CCC enrollees.

The cremated remains of most of the dead are buried in Islamorada beneath a monument to the victims that was designed by the Federal Art Project and built in 1937 by the Works Progress Administration (WPA).

World War I veterans finally got their bonus in 1936. Although FDR objected, the Senate on January 27 overrode his veto 76–19, and checks were in the mail by June.

The Great Depression (T. H. Watkins); *The Bonus Army* (Paul Dickson, Thomas Allen); *Hemingway's Hurricane* (Phil Scott); *Second Corps Area Newsletter* July 30, 1935 (Conservation Dept. files, NYS Archives); memo to Veterans Administration field officers, May 1933; memo to the president from Stephen Early, May 23, 1933 (FDR official files, FDR Library)

There were camps for "juniors"—single men aged 18 to 25. African-Americans were assigned to segregated camps. Native Americans worked on projects on or near their reservations and were allowed to live at home. Camps for veterans of any previous war, no matter their age or marital status, were added pursuant to an FDR executive order in May of 1933 (see "Camps for Veterans").

The CCC was also a major employer of loggers, carpenters, blacksmiths, tractor drivers, mechanics and other tradesmen. These "Local Experienced Men" (LEMs) were drawn from the area surrounding each camp to maintain equipment and train the green recruits on tree cutting and planting, tool use and safety. Local doctors and clergymen were also engaged to provide medical exams and treatment and to conduct worship services. A not-insignificant effect of hiring local men was to reduce resentment and increase acceptance of the camps in local communities.

Enrollees worked eight hours a day, five days a week, and could get passes on weekends to enjoy the local nightlife or go home to visit their families if they could find transportation.

Men signed up for six-month stints initially. In later years of the

New camps were often built and landscaped by their first enrollees. This was SP-133 in Margaretville.
Stanton Hogan

Wearing identical haircuts, CCC enrollees forded the Black Fork River in Utah. Many joined the CCC looking for adventure in the wilderness parks of the far west, but ended up in the somewhat tamer Catskills. Joseph Monteleone

program, they could re-up for a total of 18 months, but after that they would have to leave the CCC for six months before they were eligible to rejoin. If they found better-paying jobs on the outside closer to home, they were honorably discharged. Some couldn't take the hard physical labor or the isolation of the camps and went "over the hill," going AWOL and receiving a dishonorable discharge.

By July 1933, 275,000 young men and veterans had signed up for the CCC. A July 3 press release distributed by Fechner crowed, "More men were mobilized and transported to camps during the three months since the reforestation program was initiated than were mobilized in this country by the War Department in the first three months of American participation in the World War."

"It was a problem of the first magnitude to have supplies ready as fast as the enrollees were received," explained a 1936 yearbook for the Schenectady District of the Second Corps Area. "Army depot factories were compelled to work day and night to meet the excessive demands." Orders were placed with private concerns for clothing, shoes, boots and toilet articles, tents, kitchen ranges, cooking utensils, mess kits, lumber for the barracks and wood stoves to heat them. Trucks, vehicle parts and tools were needed, as was a supply system for delivering food and equipment to the far-flung camps.

Camp administrators also had to deal with a couple of hundred young men who suddenly found themselves in remote locations, eating, sleeping, working and brushing their teeth shoulder to shoulder with strangers from all over the country. Despite the entreaty to enrollment offices by CCC Director Fechner to select only "men who are clean-cut, purposeful, and ambitious—the finest young men that can be found," it's not surprising that enrollees were not all choir boys.

"There were illiterates and college graduates. There were 'softies' and 'hard guys.' There were men of religious inclination and those who were irreligious," said the Schenectady District yearbook. But in the main, esprit de corps was successfully cultivated among these diverse bands of young men, who also benefited physically from regular hearty meals, exercise and fresh air.

Despite the challenges he faced in dealing with so many other aspects of the Depression, FDR remained committed and involved with CCC operations. "I want personally to check on the location, scope of the camps, size, work to be done etc," he wrote in an undated memo featuring a hand-drawn management chart of the new agency, which was expanded to 350,000 men in 1934, and to 500,000 in 1935.

By then, hundreds of CCC workers had made their mark at seven camps in the Catskills region.

Racial Segregation

While the CCC rescued millions of young men from poverty and despair, it also perpetuated the racial discrimination so prevalent in society at large.

To be sure, African-American youth were accepted in the corps. The March 31, 1933, act creating the CCC barred discrimination on account of race, color or creed. However, black enrollees were usually housed in separate camps from their white counterparts, except in areas where there were not enough men of color to fill an entire company. As in the U.S. military, African-Americans were commanded by white Army officers, were largely relegated to menial jobs and were routinely prevented from rising to supervisory positions. Some white enrollees and work foremen let it be known they would refuse to work beside African-Americans.

There were several camps in New York State that were designated as "Colored." At least eight of them operated at a giant flood control project on the Wallkill River in Orange County.

Camp S-68, a mixed-race forestry camp in rural Preston, near Oxford, Chenango County, reflected the tense disparities of the era. It was the scene of a 1933 work strike resulting from the white commanding officer's replacement of two black clerical workers with white counterparts. Six enrollees were jailed, 34 workers were sent back to their homes in Harlem, and the New York State Police and an Army unit were called in because of the perceived threat of violence.

In contrast, a black company assigned to Camp SP-46 at Newtown Battlefield Reservation near Elmira exhibited a small step forward in racial equality when, in June 1937, three white men serving as commanding officer, subaltern and medical officer were replaced by black counterparts. The move, perhaps motivated by growing pressure on the Army and the CCC administration to change its policy, generated no public or press attention, unlike the disturbance at Preston.

"'A Forest Camp Disgrace': The Rebellion of Civilian Conservation Corps Workers at Preston, New York, July 7, 1933," Thomas W. Patton, *New York History*, Summer 2001; "Prejudice & Pride, The Civilian Conservation Corps at Newtown Battlefield," *The Preservationist*, Spring/Summer 2007

Chapter 4

Battling Bugs

Boiceville, Camp P-53
Ulster County
June 24, 1933–
January 10, 1936

Two months after the first CCC camp in the nation opened in Virginia on April 17, 1933, the Forest Army arrived in the Catskills to do battle with bugs.

Camp P-53 in Boiceville, the first CCC camp in the Catskills,* was occupied by an advance contingent on June 21, with the main body of 93 enrollees of Company 215 arriving four days later. The State Conservation Department intended to use the Corps as an important line of defense against the advance of the destructive gypsy moth, *Lymantria dispar,* one of North America's most devastating forest pests. (The moths lay masses of eggs on branches and trunks of trees, and the emerging larvae—caterpillars—dine on the leaves, often defoliating them.) In the 1930s, crews on Long Island were squashing egg clusters by the thousands, and the department, hoping to prevent the moth's spread to upstate forests, had set up a "barrier zone" of vigilance from the Hudson Valley to the state's eastern border.

Thus, Boiceville became known as a "bug camp" whose task was to scour 165,000 acres of state and private forest in its Ulster County environs for the gypsy moth. (The "P" in the camp's designation denotes its assignment to private lands.) With nary a moth

*During the first three weeks of June 1933, CCC camps had been established in the Adirondacks at Paul Smiths, Fish Creek Pond, Alma Farm, Speculator, Eighth Lake, and Wanakena, at Boston Corners in Columbia County, and at Goldsmith near Plattsburgh.

to be found, however, the camp's mission was broadened over the next two years to include tree planting, trail building, and clearing trees for the first mechanized ski area in New York State.

The camp was set up on six acres of land along the Esopus Creek across State Route 28 from where Onteora Central School is now located. The *Kingston Freeman* of June 22, 1933, reported that the property was leased from John and Mansfield McKelvey, who took in guests at their own camp next door. The men were first housed in platform tents before they set to work building wood frame barracks, a mess hall and other structures with the help of local carpenters. Traffic on Route 28 slowed "to take in the unfamiliar sight of a military camp in the making," the *Freeman* said. Water was first secured from the Esopus, later from a spring. Latrines were excavated, and an "evaporator" was set up to dispose of wash and wastewater. An electrical system supplied lights.

Camp P-53 was located in Boiceville between the Esopus Creek at left and State Route 28, then an undeveloped thoroughfare as evidenced in this aerial photograph. NYS Archives

By August 1933 there were 138 enrollees at work in the camp and in the woods. Major George Easterday commanded an administrative team of seven commissioned and regular Army men. Ralph R. Craner served as forestry superintendent directing a staff of 22 foremen whose job it was to train and supervise the inexperienced young men in the field. Craner made $200 a month, the other foremen $150.[1] Several enrollees, identified for their leadership potential or for special skills (clerical, for example), were chosen as "assistants" and earned $36 or $45 per month, compared to the regular monthly pay of $30.

Herb Glass, now 90, was a West Hurley teenager when he decided to sign up for the CCC. "We lived in huge tents, 20 guys to a tent, with wooden floors and canvas sides. There were outdoor showers. They gave us World War I surplus uniforms—dress wool pants and shirts—that were hotter than hell because it was summer. We paraded in Kingston on July 4, a pretty sorry lot in those uniforms."[2]

The spotless Boiceville camp was one of the earliest CCC camps established in New York.
Roy Todd

The Campground at the End of the Road

"This valley is a wander-way of sheer delight. I have yet to find a fellow tramp who has not left his heart up in Woodland Valley."

Those who have spent time tenting at Woodland Valley State Campground or hiking the rugged trails to nearby Panther, Cornell, Wittenberg or Slide Mountains, know the truth of T. Morris Longstreth's observations.

When the Catskills wanderer meandered up the six-mile valley from Phoenicia in 1916, the forest was recovering from assault by loggers and tanners in the mid-nineteenth century. The Simpson Tannery had consumed many of the hemlocks on 20,000 acres around Phoenicia. Two miles up the Valley, Col. H. D. H. Snyder opened a tannery in 1851. Though both tanneries had ceased operating long before Longstreth's walk, some scars remained, and the writer could not hide his disdain. "It is unfortunate that in this case the crimes of the fathers are visited upon the visitors. Let us hope that brimstone makes a hotter fire than brush."

The state had already acquired wounded land in the valley with an eye toward preserving it from future degradation. About 1926 it established a small campground (called "campsite" at that time) at the

The caretaker's cabin at Woodland Valley Campground was built by the CCC. Men from the Boiceville and Margaretville CCC camps worked to develop the campground. Diane Galusha

end of the road. Fireplaces, tables, benches and garbage receptacles were provided. When, in early 1933, Conservation Commissioner Lithgow Osborne asked State Senator Arthur Wicks of Kingston for suggestions on possible CCC projects in his district, the legislator happily obliged. "Enlarge and improve the existing campsite in Woodland Valley" was at the top of his list.

It appears that Company 215 at Boiceville was put to work on that project, and they got some help from Company 1230 from Margaretville. The 1935 Conservation Department Annual Report indicates that the Boiceville camp that year developed five acres of public campground, built one footbridge, four vehicle bridges, two latrines, and fourteen camp stoves or fireplaces. It also worked on a half mile of stream improvements.

Improvements continued at Woodland Valley State Campsite through 1940. Sanitary facilities, fireplaces, a water supply, and a caretaker's cabin were constructed. Margaretville's CCC company built the .4-mile road through the campsite and may have done some other work, as enrollees Lou Kole and Robert Barnes recalled traveling to Woodland Valley from Margaretville.

In 1934, the first year that attendance records were kept for Woodland Valley, 4,666 people used the site. Use increased to 6,291 in 1935, and by 1939 the number of people who came to the campground nestled amid the high peaks had increased to 8,555. This was comparable to Devil's Tombstone in Stony Clove, but well below the 16,868 who visited Beaverkill State Campsite or the 56,035 who used North Lake that year.

Conservation Department Annual Reports 1929–40; *The Catskills* (T. Morris Longstreth); *Our Catskill Mountains* (H. A. Haring); *Kingston Freeman,* June 9, 1933; interviews with Ed Ocker, Lou Kole, Robert Barnes

Glass spent just four months at Boiceville "before they found out my family wasn't on relief and they gave me an 'honorable separation.'" Meanwhile, he said, "We chased gypsy moths. We'd go through the mountains in a line, 50 men, six to eight feet between us. They'd plant fake bugs on trees with thumb tacks to train us to see them, but I don't remember ever finding a legitimate one."

Fall, winter and spring were prime time for moth-hunting. Merlin "Dutch" DuBois, now 89, recalls that each line of men would be about 25 feet through the woods from the next line, with the lead person in each line dropping slips of white paper to their right or left, marking the swath that had been examined. Then they'd turn around and separate, covering a new 25-foot strip of forest.

DuBois was the 15-year-old son of the Olive town supervisor when he and his older brother Bob were allowed to spend one summer with the CCC crew. They hitchhiked to their home in West Hurley after work every night. Work was usually in the Ulster County towns

Hearty meals were served to as many as 200 men in the Boiceville mess hall. Roy Todd

of Shandaken, Woodstock, Olive, Ulster, Hurley and Marbletown, but sometimes they went all the way to southern Schoharie County.

"We were the youngest in camp, but they treated us good," DuBois remembers. "To make a hit with the rest of the fellas, one time I bought a pack of cigarettes and passed them around in the back of the Model-A Ford truck on the ride to Gilboa."[3]

They may not have found any gypsy moths, but DuBois relishes the memory of a sweeter discovery. On the banks of the Ashokan Reservoir, where the CCC workers had been looking for egg casings on New York City lands, DuBois found a tree where wild honeybees had stored their bounty. Carving his initials in the bee tree (the traditional method of claiming it), he and an older, car-owning friend cut down the tree, which contained eight to ten feet of solid honey. It took two trips and several buckets to retrieve the estimated 100 to 200 pounds of honey.

The gypsy moth wasn't the only forest enemy confronted by the CCC workers. They also yanked gooseberry and currant bushes that harbored a fungus known as white pine blister rust, which could wreak havoc on reforestation efforts throughout the region.

Company 215's morning muster. Joseph Monteleone

Remembering Boiceville

"The CCC was like a League of Nations. We had Irish, Polish, Italians, Mexicans and Jewish in Boiceville, and two full-blooded Indians. Some read Shakespeare and played chess ... and some had problems writing their own names. ...

"We had a group that was between a hillbilly band and the Boston Pops. I was on the squeeze box. We had a harmonica, a guitar, a stiff arm fiddler and a drummer. We used to compete in amateur nights in Kingston and other places. ...

"I always found a way to make some extra money, either playing the accordion, playing baseball, or trapping muskrat and mink. I was one of two haircutters in both camps [Boiceville and Margaretville]. ...

"Most of my work consisted of building lean-tos, fireplaces and the cribbing along streams and bridges. We got a Cletrac [a crawler/tractor] from the state, and I was given the joy of driving it. It sure made work easy, hauling those logs up the mountain to build lean-tos or stones for fireplaces. ...

"When we merged with Margaretville, our group from Boiceville still came back to our own area to work. It was a 25-mile trip each way in the truck. The group from Margaretville had their own area. ... You kept a sharp eye out for copperheads and timber rattlers, especially around old quarries and rocky

Harry Collins enjoys his favorite pastime in this photo circa 1930s.
Patricia Houston

regions. We killed some copperheads, and by luck no one was ever bit by one. ...

"I held a first-aid card, so I was given a job in the infirmary [in Margaretville]. I had my own place in the infirmary and used to build benches and other odd jobs during the day, but soon got tired of it and missed the fellows and was itchy to get back in the woods. We only had two deaths in my stay in the CCC: one in Boiceville from scarlet fever, one in Margaretville from an accident while dynamiting to build a ski slope. ...

"I met my future wife [Edna Berry] in Phoenicia in 1936. We were married a few years later. I couldn't see much future in $25 a month. A forester and I got to be good friends, and his brother got me a job in Poughkeepsie. But the Catskill Mountains was still in my blood, and the Esopus, a fisherman's paradise. As time passed, I purchased a travel trailer and kept it at the Phoenicia trailer park, and spent most weekends and vacations there."

From a memoir written in 1990 by Harry T. Collins and provided by his granddaughter, Patricia Houston

"They took 'em right out of people's yards, too. A lot of people didn't like it," recalled former enrollee Barnet Howland of Shady in a 1996 interview.[4] The effort to eradicate blister rust continued into the 1940s when some former CCC members returned to the woods to help the Conservation Department with this ambitious undertaking.

The Conservation Department soon found other tasks for the fit young men. Development of Woodland Valley Campsite was one of them. (See "The Campground at the End of the Road.")

Ed Ocker of Shandaken remembered building log docking as flood control devices in Birch Creek and in Broadstreet Hollow, Fox Hollow and Esopus Creeks. An inspector's report on the camp filed with the Emergency Conservation Work (ECW) office prior to the first winter of the camp's operation predicted, "It would be difficult for men to work here during the winter by reason of heavy snow which would require snow shoes."[5]

But work they did. "In winter we stacked logs for the coming spring and shoveled snow around the camp," Ocker said. He also recalled building an observation tower on Slide Mountain, the highest peak in the Catskills.[6] The 47-foot tower was erected in 1934, according to the Conservation Department annual report for that year.

When weather allowed, the men of Camp 53 planted trees. The Kanape Brook area, where the state had acquired marginal farm-lands, was reforested by the Boiceville boys.[7] They did other work, too. The 1936 Annual Report of the Conservation Department showed that Camp 53 built one trailside shelter and five miles of foot trails. They spent 103 man-days helping to fight forest fires, and 221 man-days on fire suppression (building access roads and fire ponds, and clearing dead trees and underbrush). A total of 17,376 acres of forest were examined for gypsy moth and blister rust infestation.

Martin Eckert, left, traded his illegal brew to CCC staff for staples from the Boiceville camp kitchen. Bud Eckert has his father's home-made still, bearing the axe slashes of the revenue agents. Bud Eckert

Trees banded against gypsy moth infestation. Boiceville was known as a "bug camp," its enrollees scouring the forests for signs of the defoliating caterpillar. NYS Conservation Department 1940 Annual Report

One of the most intensive jobs undertaken by the Boiceville company, and by the Margaretville CCC company, was the clearing of trails for the Jay Simpson Memorial Ski Slope on the road to Woodland Valley outside Phoenicia. (See "Ski Fever.")

Not everyone thrived on this kind of manual labor. In the first months of operation, nine "elopements" were recorded among enrollees "who had no desire for work." Thirteen more were dishonorably discharged because of their "refusal to work." There was, in fact, a tough element among the enrollees from all over the state who'd been tossed together in Boiceville. "I think the CCC kept some of them out of prison," quipped Ed Ocker.

When not in the field, the young men enjoyed a range of recreational and educational activities. Michael Frohlich was the educational advisor who found instructors to teach classes in spelling and arithmetic, Spanish and photography, shorthand and letter writing. Frohlich himself led sessions on "Getting a Job" and "Current Events." Classes were offered from 5:30 to 9:00 PM and were followed by meetings of the stamp, photography, radio and cartooning clubs.[8]

A library of 450 volumes offered mysteries, plays, short stories and popular tales of the Wild West and adventure, like Zane

Grey's *Riders of the Purple Sage* and Lowell Thomas's *With Lawrence in Arabia.*[9]

A dance in October 1934 drew a big crowd of townspeople to hear a local combo and "the camp's own Hill-Billy band." There were inter-barracks talent competitions and, in the spring of 1935, "Camp Follies" including a chorus line, skits and music.[10] The *Kingston Freeman* of July 9, 1935, said Horace Gardner, who had been associated with Lee and J. J. Schubert, the New York Theater Guild and George M. Cohan, was at the camp for the summer as dramatic instructor. He directed the enrollees in skits, minstrel shows and theatrical productions, and coordinated construction of a stage in the recreation hall with scenery "made for the purpose in New York City." An orchestra and a fife and drum band were also organized.

Sports were popular, of course. A gym in nearby Chichester was used for basketball games where a six-foot-seven center led the Boiceville team against visitors from other Hudson Valley camps. Dances followed the Friday night contests. Baseball, volleyball and boxing were other diversions.[11]

The Boiceville camp was landscaped and lighted. Eric Fedde

Enrollees were also free to seek their own entertainment on weekends. Leroy Winchell recalled seeing CCC workers with their thumbs out in front of the camp on Route 28 looking for rides to Kingston.[12]

Keeping the men healthy was a task left to the cooks and to the local doctors contracted to treat the enrollees when they fell ill. "Menus are well balanced. Fresh fruits, fresh vegetables, Grade A steer beef and milk are served," reported the camp inspector on April 2, 1935. "Average gain in weight of enrollees from time of entry to separation, 12 lbs." The Army Commissary at Fort Jay provided most of the staples; perishables were purchased in Kingston.

Transactions of another sort took place under the radar, according to Bud Eckert of Shokan. His father, Martin, carried on some creative bartering with the camp kitchen staff. The elder Eckert collected mess hall scraps to feed the 30 hogs he raised on his small farm in Watson Hollow, where he also kept a still for making illegal whiskey. He would pick up the garbage in barrels each week, and when he returned them, he'd leave a gallon of apple jack in one of them, buried beneath some scraps to make it look as if he'd just forgotten to empty it. "On the next load out, he'd find a gallon of peaches, or honey, or a ham. There'd always be a few goodies in trade," explained his son. "They never got caught at it, either."[13]

Sickness occasionally ran through the camp like wildfire. Local diarist Elwyn Davis noted on January 19, 1934, that "the Boiceville CCC camp with all its personnel is shut down tonight with a scarlet fever quarantine." He noted two more cases of the disease at the camp in May.

Serious injuries and surgeries were handled at Fort Jay. In April 1934 the mother of a Schenectady enrollee who had been injured at Camp 53 while piling lumber, wrote to President Roosevelt requesting recompense for the nine months of work he anticipated losing while recuperating from what she called

The late Ed Ocker, shown in the cabin of the Slide Mountain fire tower as a CCC enrollee, and in his Shandaken home in 2007, worked at both the Boiceville and Margaretville camps. Ed Ocker; Diane Galusha

"unnecessary" surgery at Army doctors' hands. The letter was referred to the Army, whose response is not known.[14]

Camp 53 was plunged into mourning in March 1935 when Lt. Otto Wienecke, a camp commander from its inception, was killed in a plane crash. Wienecke, an aviator with more than 1,200 hours in the air, had recently been recalled to service with the Army Air Corps, which FDR had ordered to begin carrying the mail because of a collusion scandal among three commercial air mail carriers. Ten pilots were killed in crashes during the first three weeks of the Army's takeover of the service. Four of them, including Wienecke who flew his Curtis Falcon into an Ohio cornfield in a snowstorm, died on a single day—March 9, 1935.

Wienecke had been a respected leader. The name of the camp's newspaper, *Camp Wienecke News*, reflected his popularity among the enrollees who had only recently watched him perform loops and rolls in his Air Corps plane above Boiceville.

Anxiety gripped the camp again in late winter of 1935 when the future of the CCC was being debated on the national stage.

Controversy over the "experimental social security program" had held up passage of an appropriations bill to continue work relief programs and to double the size of the CCC. By early April, with funding still not approved, enrollees and local foremen were given the choice of going home or continuing to work without a paycheck and no guarantee of a settlement over the impasse.[15]

But most had no prospects at home, either. The number of New Yorkers added to home relief or work relief rolls, or both, in January 1935 was up by 4 percent, to a total of 562,165. After five years of the Depression, even those who had managed thus far to stay off relief rolls "found their resources finally exhausted."[16] Former CCC enrollee William Ward of Utica, back in the job market after completing a maximum 18 months in the Boiceville camp, advised his former mates to stay where they were. "I have not succeeded in securing employment although I have tried very hard," he wrote to Education Coordinator Michael Frohlich on Feb. 22, 1935. "There are jobs out there, but only the experienced men get them. ... The feature [about camp] that I liked best was that I was always able to be busy. I was able to earn my own way. I miss being out of doors, even though hunting the elusive Gypsy Moth is not the best kind of inspiring work to do."

Concluded Ward, "I hope the President revises the entrance regulations. I would be one of the ex-CCCers who would readily rejoin. I think there are many in the same boat. We are young, willing to work, but have no vocation to follow."[17]

Indeed, the bill was signed and the CCC expanded its work, adding 36 new forestry and state park companies in New York. The Soil Conservation Service was brought on board to set up erosion control camps, and 18 companies were to work on a massive flood control project on the Wallkill River under the auspices of the Army Corps of Engineers.[18]

Unidentified CCC men work atop Slide Mountain, where the Boiceville company erected a 47-foot observation tower in 1934. Stanton Hogan

And so, Boiceville's "bug camp" hung on for the remainder of 1935, though there were questions about whether it had outlived its usefulness. Special Investigator Charles Kenlan, who had given glowing reports to his bosses at the Emergency Conservation Work headquarters on the camp's physical, educational, and social amenities, wrote on April 2 to ECW Assistant Director James McIntee seeking a review of Camp S-53's work purpose (the "S" in the designation now reflected its greater concentration on state, rather than private, lands).

Noting that no gypsy moths had been discovered in two years of looking, and that the moth crew had been reduced to 25 men (total enrollment of the company was down to 128), Kenlan

Celebrating Conservation

The year 1935 marked the fiftieth anniversary of the establishment of the Catskill and Adirondack Forest Preserves, an occasion for a look back in the Conservation Department's Annual Report for 1935:

> On May 15, 1885, Governor David B. Hill signed a bill setting aside a little more than 700,000 acres of land in the Adirondack and Catskill mountains as a permanent preserve and constituting a Forest Commission to care for and develop this area. Much of this land had been cut over by lumbermen and abandoned, and had reverted to the state because of failure to pay taxes upon it. ...
>
> From this original state preserve has grown the whole conservation movement in New York. The Forest Preserve of 1935 contains more than 2,350,000 acres, 95 percent of it covered with trees. Thus more than half of the two principal mountain areas of the State of New York are assured of perpetual forests protecting the water supply, encouraging the continuance of wild life and providing a vast recreation region for the people.

The old impulse to conquer the wilderness must now be changed to saving it, the report said. The fiftieth anniversary celebration made apparent "the necessity of salvaging the considerable portion of natural wealth which remains to them and in rebuilding a great part of that which their ancestors so thoughtlessly destroyed."

The major celebration was a three-day rally of conservationists and sportsmen at Lake Placid on September 12–14, featuring appearances by President Roosevelt, Governor Herbert Lehman and other dignitaries.

Regional events were held all summer long, including a July 4 bash at Schoharie sponsored by the local board of trade and ten conservation clubs in the county. The parade attracted 10,000 spectators, but stepped off an hour late because of the reluctance of a four-legged participant to join the party.

"A live coon which was to ride on the float of the Middleburg Rod & Gun Club escaped to a tree and it was some time before it could be brought down. On the same float was a coon dog. It was easily seen why Mr. Coon was afraid to ride."

The float won second prize. First place went to a Boy Scouts float showing the impact of fire on a green forest.

A small lake formed by Bushnellsville Creek in Westkill Notch, 1919, when the state was actively purchasing land in the Catskills to preserve it for posterity. NYS Archives

suggested that McIntee look into "whether it is desirable to proceed further on this class of work in this section."

McIntee passed the problem on to C. M. Granger, acting chief of the U.S. Forest Service, who replied on June 3 that "the expenditure of a large number of man-days in the discovery of relatively few egg clusters seems to be inevitable" in such a preventative project and, in fact, is "justified by the objectives of the enterprise."[19]

Camp 53 had once again dodged the bullet. But while the need for work relief continued, the expanded CCC was having a hard time meeting its enrollment quotas. Eligibility was extended to those aged 17 to 28, with no limit to the amount of time one could remain. Late in 1935 plans were in the works to reduce the strength of the CCC nationwide from 600,000 to 500,000 by July 1, 1936. Camps were being closed, companies consolidated.[20]

On December 21, 1935, superintendents of 12 camps in New York State got an unwelcome Christmas present in the form of a telegram from federal officials telling them to close up shop by the first of the year. Camp S-53 in Boiceville was among them.

"The work projected for these 12 camps is not finished but they are the ones whose loss we will feel the least," explained Lithgow Osborne, the state's conservation commissioner. He pointed out that one of the camps to close was in his home county of Cayuga. Though it was named Camp Osborne in his honor, it was not spared the axe.[21]

In early January, 125 CCC workers packed their gear and vacated the Boiceville camp. Forty-two of the men headed to Camp S-133 in Margaretville, 51 went to Camp S-97 in Tannersville, and 14 others were transferred to P-83 in Boston Corners near what is now Taconic State Park. On January 10, 1936, after two and a half years of operation, Camp S-53 was officially closed and a caretaker was hired to watch over the site until it could be dismantled.[22]

What actually became of the various camp buildings is unclear. At least one of the structures remained standing for many years. It was used as a storage building by the Town of Olive until it was torn down in 1959 to make room for the service station that now occupies the site.[23]

CHAPTER 5
OF BLISTER RUST
AND FIRE TOWERS

DAVENPORT, CAMP S-51
DELAWARE COUNTY
JUNE 29, 1933–
NOVEMBER 11, 1933

Like the CCC enrollees in Boiceville, the boys of Camp S-51 were assigned the task of protecting the state's investment in new plantations on abandoned farmlands in the area where three Delaware County towns—Davenport, Kortright and Harpersfield—intersect.

While Boiceville looked for bugs, Davenport scouted the woods and fields for gooseberry and currant bushes, carriers of white pine blister rust. They ranged over a 25-mile radius, ripping out the so-called "ribes." But in the four months of the camp's operation, crews also constructed the base of a fire tower in nearby Stamford and installed a telephone line to another in the Town of Tompkins.

An advance contingent of 25 members of Company 211, along with five Army leaders under the command of Hans C. Jespersen arrived from Fort Wadsworth on Staten Island to set up the new camp. It was located on the McArthur farm, about 200 yards off NYS Route 23 in the vicinity of the confluence of Teedle Brook and Middle Brook. Situated in a "perfect sylvan setting on a plateau," the tent camp was set up in a matter of hours, according to a June 27 newspaper account.

Tents have been erected in street formation at the rear of the camp site. Board floors protect the occupants from wet weather and soil moisture. At the front entrance to the camp are the officers' quarters, also in a large tent. Nearby is the cook tent. Here an outdoor stove and pit for cooking and baking is in use. Near mealtime, savory odors are wafted across the camp on the breeze. A corps of cooks works under the direction of a chef.

Gangs of men engaged in excavation burrow like so many power shovels. One crew rests while another wields picks and shovels. A general atmosphere of cheerfulness prevails.[1]

Another 64 men, fresh from training at Fort Dix, New Jersey, arrived within the week on a New York Central Catskill Mountain Branch train to Oneonta to help build a water tower, a ten-head shower house and a screened-in cook shack. An electric light plant was established, and a septic tank installed for kitchen waste. By early July there were 110 enrollees, many of them from Delaware, Chenango, Otsego and Greene Counties, working under the direction of Noble Harp of the State Conservation Department, with guidance from 20 "Local Experienced Men" (LEMs).[2]

Predictably, some enrollees left because of homesickness or "unwillingness to work," so area men flocked to the Oneonta Armory to sign up. If they passed the physical, they were taken immediately to Davenport. Ultimately, there were 230 men, including enrollees, LEMs, Conservation Department staff and Army personnel.*

It didn't take long for the young workers to discover the natural amenities of the site, building a dam to create a swimming hole on Middle Brook. It was a popular place on the hottest days during that busy summer of 1933.[3] A call for donations of

---

*The local press also reported on area men who'd been shipped to camps in Montana, and on company movements through the rail hub of Oneonta, which in June of 1933 saw three trains bearing 999 enrollees and officers, fresh from training in Plattsburgh, headed for camps in Idaho.

Camp S-51 was a collection of platform tents that housed Company 211 in Davenport for six months in 1933. NYS Archives

used bathing suits, along with old magazines, jigsaw puzzles, and books, was issued through the local press.[4]

Men gathered during their off hours at a camp recreation hall and canteen where they could spend the $5 a month they kept from their $30 paychecks. They organized ball teams to do battle against CCC brethren at other camps in the region. They saw movies that circulated among the camps. And they occasionally staged their own entertainments, such as the minstrel show reported by the *Oneonta Daily Star* on September 27, 1933, that included "singing, tap dancing and blackface acts."

When it was learned that the camp had no American flag (at $9 each, the government did not initially purchase flags for the hundreds of CCC camps across the country), a member of the Oneonta Chapter of the Daughters of the American Revolution found a World War veteran, Robert L. Johnson of Oneonta, to donate one. A stone base was constructed for a flagpole, and the flag was raised with Civil War veteran Clinton Ford in attendance. Afterward, flag raising and lowering ceremonies were conducted at the camp.[5]

While the focus of Company 211's work was on blister rust control, some of its members were employed in fire tower construction.

CCC crews from Davenport and from Camp SP-11 at Gilbert Lake State Park in Laurens, Otsego County, combined efforts in the summer of 1933 to begin construction of a fire tower on 2,300-foot Rock Rift Mountain in the Town of Tompkins. The job included constructing a three-mile road to the tower and installing a telephone line.[6] The tower was completed in 1934 by Company 211 after it moved from Davenport to a new camp, P-76, in McClure, Broome County. The 1935 NYS Conservation Department Report to the Legislature recorded that 12 fires were spotted from the Rock Rift tower in its first full season of operation. The 68-foot steel tower was used by the state through the 1980s. It is still owned by the state, but the land surrounding it is now the property of New York City, whose Cannonsville Reservoir is nearby.[7]

The camp was situated on the MacArthur farm in the Town of Davenport. NYS Archives

In the fall of 1933, Davenport men were trucked to Mt. Utsayan-tha in Stamford where the state was building a steel fire tower to replace a wooden one. The Davenport CCC crew poured the con-crete footings for the 68-foot tower and erected 20 feet of the steel work. Comrades from the Breakabeen CCC camp finished the tower the following year.[8] The observation site atop the 3,200-foot mountain welcomed hundreds of visitors in 1934, and its fire war-den reported 14 fires from the tower's cab in 1935.[9]

By September 1933 the blister rust work had diminished enough so that a crew of only 12 was removing ribes. "The major-ity of the company is engaged in tree planting in the vicinity of Masonville," reported the *Oneonta Daily Star* on September 3. "Five truck loads of men commute to and from work daily." On Sep-tember 13 the paper reported on a curious project: "mosquito research." This was "part of a nationwide mosquito survey carried

Trucks loaded with men prepare to search area fields for gooseberry bushes, which carried a disease damaging to white pines that were being planted by the thousands on reforesta-tion tracts throughout the region. NYS Archives

on by CCC camps. A few specimens were caught at the Davenport camp and have been sent to the Army medical museum."

The Conservation Department Annual Report for 1933 also reported that Davenport CCC workers constructed three miles of truck trails, planted 1,570 acres of trees, scouted 6,910 acres for blister rust carriers, and installed five miles of telephone line. Six million trees were slated for planting that season by the Davenport and McDonough CCC camps.

August Basani was a teenager, one of nine children of Italian immigrant parents living on the family farm down the road from the Davenport camp in the summer of 1933. He watched as truckloads of workers drove back and forth to job sites and recalled that he and his siblings, and the family dog, would be welcomed by the camp's cooks when the CCC workers were off planting trees or building towers. "We'd go in the kitchen and

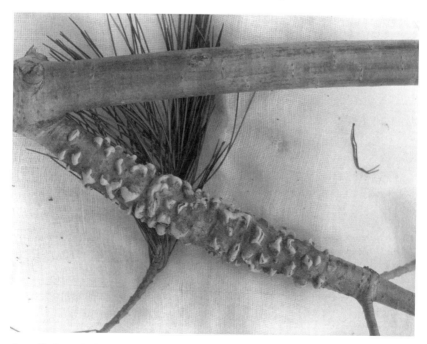

A conifer branch showing blister rust. NYS Archives

Gilbert Lake: A State Park Grows

While the State Conservation Department was using Davenport CCC enrollees to combat white pine blister rust, the State Parks Commission was employing them to expand Gilbert Lake State Park in Laurens, Otsego County.

The park had been established in 1926 on 1,550 acres of marginal farmland the state had acquired. But by the time the Depression set in, it was still barely more than a lake with a few campsites. The availability of the Civilian Conservation Corps ensured its development as a premiere park in central New York.

Camp SP-11 (the SP designated a camp devoted to work in a State Park) was first set up in late June 1933 five miles away from Gilbert Lake, on the Dutcher farm on the Oneonta–Mt. Vision road. Administrators feared that an influx of 200 "raw recruits," most of them from New York City and New Jersey and "unaccustomed to taking orders or working together," would scare away the few campers who were coming to the new park.

"Reports from other camps concerning minor disorders led people to believe that situations of this nature were common in all camps," explained the *Oneonta Daily Star*. The newcomers instead exhibited

The CCC-built pavilion on the beach at Gilbert Lake State Park was a popular place in the 1930s, and so it remains.
NYS CCC Museum

Enrollees at SP-11 built a 21-cabin tourist compound at Gilbert Lake, using local timber milled onsite. NYS CCC Museum

"excellent discipline" and "earned the right to move into the park." By July 14 the members of Company 212 occupied a new tent city within the park itself. (*The Whistle,* the camp newspaper, said in a 1937 article looking back at the company's accomplishments, that the move was made because there was an inadequate water supply on the Dutcher farm.)

During the company's eight-year tenure at Gilbert Lake, it built a 21-cabin colony for tourist lodging, each cabin made from local timber cut on the camp's own sawmill. The cabins were wired and plumbed, and the furniture was made by the enrollees, who also built dozens of campsites with fireplaces. They built service and caretaker buildings and seven shelters that bear the distinct stone and timber design common to many CCC-built facilities across the country and still enjoyed by park-goers today.

Company 212 created a lakeside beach, bathhouse and docks, constructed maintenance buildings and built roads, parking areas and extensive walking and bridle paths. The company even built a small wildlife refuge consisting of three ponds for waterfowl and a herd of 11 deer kept in a 12-acre fenced yard.

There was extensive clearing of dead and diseased trees, tree planting and landscaping throughout the park.

In 1934 Company 212 built an 80-foot steel fire tower atop a 1,790-foot hill at the park and staffed it through the autumn of 1941. (In 1948 the state moved the tower to Leonard Hill in Schoharie County.) The Gilbert Lake CCC workers also helped build the Rock Rift fire tower and access road in the Town of Tompkins in 1933 and 1934, and responded to severe regional flooding in 1935 by sending crews to help residents of Unadilla and Delhi.

Camp SP-11 was a vibrant place, with its own orchestra, newspaper, and an active educational program. Boxing, ping-pong, baseball, track and field, and craft activities were popular. There were monthly dances (girls were trucked in from the Oneonta area) and movies every other week.

Bill Ronovech and his brother Chuck both enrolled at Gilbert Lake. "When I graduated from high school in 1934, you couldn't buy a job," Bill recalled. "The CCC certainly was a blessing to me and my family." He was the manager of the camp baseball team, which one year captured the state-wide crown in a round-robin tournament of 12 CCC camps. "I'll never forget it. I cherish those years," he said.

As the nation emerged from the Depression, and the economy improved with the coming of World War II, Company 212 had a hard time attracting enrollees. On August 7, 1941, SP-11 at Gilbert Lake, one of the last CCC camps in New York State, was closed.

The park now houses the New York State CCC Museum, which is open from Memorial Day to Labor Day (www.nyscccmuseum.com).

Oneonta Daily Star (several articles from 1933); "Civilian Conservation Corps Camp SP-11, Company 212, Gilbert Lake State Park" (1985 historical paper at New York State Room, Huntington Library, Oneonta); The Whistle, April 1937; Fire Towers of the Catskills, Their History and Lore (Marty Podskoch); interview with Bill Ronovech March 22, 2008

The Rock Rift fire observation tower, built by men from the Davenport and Laurens CCC camps and completed in 1934, is shown surrounded by the forest it was constructed to protect. NYS Archives

they'd give us steak and other stuff, even the dog," he remembered in a 2007 interview.

By autumn the government was struggling with the dilemma of which camps to winterize, which to vacate, and where new camps should be developed to take on new and larger conservation assignments. Davenport's tent city was ordered removed. Of the 18 camps opened in New York State in May and June 1933 to do work overseen by the Conservation Department,* 13 were closed as the first chill winds of winter whistled through their tents. Eleven new camps were established, including one at McClure, near Deposit, on the western edge of Delaware County. This is where Company 211 headed after folding the tents of Davenport Camp S-51. [10]

*Four other CCC camps opened in early 1933 were overseen by the State Parks Commission to expand four recently established parks: Gilbert Lake, Green Lakes, Selkirk Shores and Chenango Valley.

Back on July 17, when Company 211 had been at work for just three weeks, President Roosevelt spoke to CCC workers in a nationwide address. A radio set was reportedly installed at each camp so that the boys—300,000 of them by now—could hear themselves described as "a visible token of encouragement to the whole country. ... You are evidence that we are seeking to get away as fast as we possibly can from soup kitchens and free rations, because the government is paying you for actual work, work which is needed now and for the future and will bring a definite financial return to the people of the nation.

"It is time for each and every one of us to cast away self-destroying, nation-destroying efforts to get something for nothing, to appreciate that satisfying reward and safe reward come only through honest work. That must be the new spirit of the American future. You are the vanguard of that new spirit."[11]

The camp was struck in late 1933 and the company moved to McClure.
Davenport Historical Society

CHAPTER 6

DOING THE
DIRTY WORK

DEPOSIT/McCLURE
CAMP P-76
BROOME COUNTY
NOVEMBER 11, 1933–
OCTOBER 18, 1935

O n an August afternoon in 1934, a truckload of CCC boys with supervisors Jack Odell and W. W. Knowlton, returning to Deposit Camp P-76 from a day of hunting for gypsy moths, was flagged down by a motorist who had spotted a cow mired in a swamp near the McClure Creamery.

Twenty guys went to the rescue of the bleating bovine. It was a messy scene, as reported in the next issue of the camp newspaper: "The boys pulled and pushed, tugged and heaved. The swamp oozed; the cow lurched; mud flew in many directions, principally at the boys. Finally, all hands grunting under the strain, enrollee Hendricksen gave the tail the right degree of twist and up and out came Mrs. Bossy."[1] The *Deposit Courier* of August 9 said the cow's release brought cheers from a crowd of concerned onlookers. "Brushing off their hands as they climbed back on the truck, the boys informed the spectators it was all in a day's work, and rolled off to a late supper."

The men of Camp 76 were called on to perform such dirty work several times during their two-year stay in McClure, near Deposit. In May 1935, they helped clean up at the scene of an accident in which a truck loaded with 100 cases of eggs and 10 crates of live chickens careened over an embankment.[2] That dry spring, they battled two brush and forest fires, and in summer helped mud- and water-logged Southern Tier residents recover from a devastating flood.

Their efforts gained them community goodwill and recognition, and provided diversions from the mundane task of bug-hunting, which was so monotonous that several enrollees had gone "over the hill."[3] But by the time Camp 76 closed in the fall of 1935, its occupants could point to a number of more tangible accomplishments, including more than two million trees on the landscape and two fire towers to help protect them.

The camp was constructed by workers from the Deposit area over a six-week period in the fall of 1933 while Company 211 was still at Davenport. On November 11, Captain Hans Jespersen accompanied 112 young men from Davenport to the new camp along Route 17 in the Town of Sanford, Broome County. Land for the camp had been rented from farmer Leon Smith. It was two and a half miles west of the Village of Deposit, 30 miles east of Binghamton.[4]

It was a great improvement over the tent camp they had occupied in Davenport where, one veteran recalled, "as the weather grew colder, Sibley stoves were put in the tents, more blankets and even overcoats were piled on the bunks, and [outdoor] showers became the privilege of only the hardiest."[5]

This was Company #211 in May of 1935 at Camp P-76 in McClure, near Deposit.
Indian Hills Girl Scout Council

Ancillary buildings at the new camp were completed by December 1934. Twelve structures, including four barracks, a mess hall, recreation hall, infirmary, garages and storage buildings, comprised the camp. Water was taken from Oquaga Creek, but it was of such poor quality it had to be heavily chlorinated.

In January 1934, Captain Jespersen was reassigned and Army Reservist Werner Strecker assumed command of the facility. John ("Jack") Odell of the U.S. Department of Agriculture's Forest Service was in charge of conservation projects and of a dozen foremen who supervised the boys as they worked.[6]

The camp was initially charged with looking for gypsy moths and white pine blister rust carriers on an area covering more than 10,000 acres of private land (thus the P in the camp's numerical designation). By November the company had scouted

The McClure camp is shown in this aerial photograph depicting treeless hillsides ripe for reforestation. NYS Archives

391 miles of roadside and 59,050 acres of woodland looking for moth casings on 98,791 shade trees and 33,878 fruit trees. They concentrated their search for gooseberry and currant bushes (known as "ribes") in areas of white pine concentrations, covering 10,831 acres of land and destroying more than a quarter million bushes.[7]

From June to September 1935, the men continued the hunt for ribes in the Towns of Colesville, Sanford, Windsor, Bainbridge and Masonville.[8] Crews from the camp fought a stubborn forest fire in May on the Frank Fineout farm on Tarbell Hill, a mile from Deposit. Thirty-mile-per-hour wind gusts fanned flames over 20 acres of brush and timber, according to the *Deposit Courier* of May 10, 1935. It took 50 CCC workers, under the direction of Forest Ranger Harvey Bump and Fire Warden Albert Hammett, four hours to douse the blaze.

Separate crews were set to work planting trees. Lots of them. Between April 18 and May 31, 1934, they planted 2,270,000 tree seedlings on state-owned lands, a record for New York State CCC camps that spring.[9] The company's productivity helped win the camp top prize honors among 34 camps in the state for the six months of April 1 through September 30, 1934. The award was based largely on the amount and quality of the work accomplished, but also on morale ("cheerfulness, energy and willingness of enrollees to volunteer for work on their off days"), on care of equipment, camp appearance and on the average percentage of men actually engaged in forestry work (79 percent in McClure's case, the rest designated as retained for camp duty, sick, on leave or AWOL).[10]

The company didn't rest on its laurels, however. After finishing the Rock Rift fire tower and access road (see Chapter 5), Company 211 began a similar tower at nearby Page Pond in the Town of Sanford. The 1934 Conservation Department Annual Report indicates they built the foundation that year, and the camp newspaper celebrated its completion in 1935. Large expanses of State Forest could be seen from the 80-foot tower atop the 2,040-foot hill. The state manned it with fire watchers through 1988.[11] Completion of the road to the tower, through adjacent Girl Scout Camp Amahami, had to wait until early fall of 1935 because all hands of Company 211 were called to a different kind of public service—flood relief.[12]

When rain began falling on Sunday, July 7, 1935, farmers and gardeners in the Southern Tier and western Catskills breathed a sigh of relief that a long dry spell was over. But the gentle showers turned into a torrential downpour that evening, dumping eight inches of rain in 12 hours and provoking a flood that reporters said was the worst since 1865.

Forty-three people died and 255 were injured in the flooding, which swept away 142 homes and damaged more than 9,000 others. Thousands of people in eight counties were left homeless and the Red Cross was hard-pressed to feed and shelter them all.[13] Communities along the West Branch of the Delaware River and along the Susquehanna River were inundated. Businesses were knocked out, roads and bridges destroyed, barns and pastures left awash in mud and debris.

CCC camps in the vicinity of flooded towns were called upon to help dig out basements and clear farm fields of debris. Company 211 set up a temporary camp at Whitney Point to be closer to work details in the Towns of Whitney Point, Lisle and other stricken areas in Broome County.

"The general public had a rather vague idea as to the purpose of the CCC and the type of youth and man making up its personnel," acknowledged Jesse Huffman of the City of Binghamton Welfare Office in a July 22 letter of thanks to Camp 76. "No question now exists in their minds because of the valor and bravery which was displayed under stress of emergency. ... We may all thank the Lord that we had the CCC companies located so stra-

The 80-foot Page Pond fire observation tower was built by Company 211 after it moved from Davenport to McClure. The tower was manned until 1988 and is on property of Camp Amahami Girl Scout Camp.
Bob Eckler

tegically throughout the entire flood area. Without such an organization we certainly would have had a great loss of lives and far greater loss of property."[14]

Merchants in the Deposit area certainly recognized the value of the CCC in their midst. The business community greeted the company with open arms and a front page welcome advertisement in the *Deposit Courier* on November 23, 1933. "We hope you will consider this your home town during your stay at camp on Route 17," the ad said, noting that while many of the merchants listed would offer discounts to CCC workers, "we wish you to understand that you are welcome whether or not you have any money to spend."

CCC boys engage in the search for currant and gooseberry bushes, bearers of white pine blister rust, in this photo from the 1933 Conservation Department Annual Report.

Local folks responded to the camp's call for furniture for its recreation hall. Curtains for the barracks were sewn by members of the Daughters of the American Revolution, Red Cross, Daughters of Union Veterans, the Fortnightly Club, the American Legion Auxiliary and all five Deposit churches. Auxiliary members relieved KP crews on Sundays, preparing, serving and cleaning up after dinner. Area libraries and residents donated books and magazines to the camp library.

Company 211 led an active sports and social life. The 1934 baseball team won 13 out of 15 games against nine other camps in its CCC league. The team's pitcher, Paul Pendleton, was selected to the "All American CCC Star Baseball Team" by the national CCC publication Happy Days.[15]

The camp's seven-member Hill-Billy Band played for camp dances and, in December of 1934, performed at the Windsor Town Hall along with a troupe of youthful Binghamton vaudeville entertainers.[16]

A Binghamton enrollee, Nicholas Piros, brought his knowledge of shortwave radio to the camp, where he set up 35-watt Station W8YMR for broadcasting messages and emergency announcements. The unit successfully contacted Australia, Spain, Italy, the Panama Canal Zone and 44 states.[17]

Classes in practical mathematics and surveying, physics, auto and airplane mechanics, vocational guidance and practical science and hygiene (required) were offered to enrollees by Educational Advisor L. E. Green. A model airplane club was established. An average of 35 enrollees was transported to village churches each Sunday, and others attended services offered by clergymen at the camp itself.

Occasionally, entertainment came to them, as in September 1935 when "Pitroff, the Clowning Magician with his Humpty Dumpty Circus and Midget Marionettes" made an appearance, according to Bugs and Blisters. The camp newspaper also reported sadder news. Its February 21, 1935, issue contained an article about the death of Binghamton enrollee Harold Addington, assistant editor of the paper, in a car accident on Route 17. Superintendent Strecker used the article to remind the rest of the company that it was against regulations for enrollees to have a car. (Addington had kept his hidden away from camp.)

If they weren't planting trees, CCC men were thinning woodlots or searching for tree pests and disease carriers. Joseph Monteleone

Veggies by the Ton

Impoverished young men accepted for work in the CCC often arrived undernourished. Some signed up just for the promised three square meals a day. Once they were put to work at hard physical labor, it was all mess hall staffs could do to satisfy their hunger.

The menu for a week in March 1934 at Camp P-76 was typical of most CCC camps. Breakfast offerings included scrambled eggs, cereal, potato pancakes and French toast. Weekday lunches provided in the field featured several kinds of sandwiches, fresh fruit and cookies or cake. Dinner was veal cutlets and creamed peas, mackerel loaf and sweet potatoes, corned beef hash and buttered beets, and on Sundays, cold cuts and leftovers.

The February 1935 issue of the McClure camp's newspaper, *Bugs and Blisters*, listed the staggering quantities of food consumed by 200 men every week:

1 ton of vegetables	32 large cans of jam
700 pounds of bread	661 pounds of meat
150 pounds of oatmeal	1½ gallons of ketchup
600 boxes of dry cereal	130 pounds of coffee and
1,800 eggs	cocoa
1,375 bottles of milk	300 pounds of flour
6 bushels of apples	6 gallons of pickles
97 gallons of canned fruit	

Concluded the report, "It makes you wonder how the handful of men in the kitchen manage to turn it out on time all ready to eat when the whistle blows."

As many as 40 men lived in the typical barracks building, like this one at Breakabeen.
Ruth Dietz

Several camp physicians looked after enrollees' health. Responding to rumors that a scarlet fever epidemic was spreading through the camp, Health Officer Dr. Clayton M. Axtell reported through the *Deposit Courier* on March 22, 1934, that an examination of the men showed no signs of the disease. A measles outbreak the following March, however, quarantined 40 men.[18]

As the first anniversary of the McClure camp approached in the autumn of 1934, Superintendent Strecker declared November 11 to be "an outstanding day for a birthday," coinciding as it did with Armistice Day, which marked the end of World War I. On that day 16 years earlier, Strecker had been a corporal in Company I, 29th Engineers, stationed in Langres-Houte-Marne, France. After the war, he'd gotten a job at GE in Schenectady, but lost it in 1931 when the Depression hit home. A Reserve Army officer, he was assigned to active duty in September 1933 and joined Company 211 in Davenport. He'd accompanied the men to McClure and had been their commanding officer since January 1934.

Captain Strecker and his company enjoyed a celebratory dinner of scalloped oysters on November 11, 1934. There would not be a second anniversary.

News that Company 211 was moving again, this time to Elmsford, Westchester County, was greeted with dismay by the Deposit

Company 211 helped Southern Tier residents clean up from devastating floods in 1935. This photo shows Laurens CCC members doing the same. NYS CCC Museum

community. "It is the earnest wish of the people of Deposit, with few exceptions, that another camp will be located here in the near future. We are sorry to see the boys leave. They have made many friends in town and have never given local people any trouble," said the *Deposit Courier* on October 17, 1935. "Many people here never realized until it was thought the camp was leaving how much the CCC has meant to Deposit business concerns. Not all, but many, have benefited directly by trading with the campers, foresters and officers.* Those who did not benefit directly, could not help but benefit indirectly, in one way or another."

By the time those words saw print, Company 211 had moved on to Elmsford, and Camp P-76 was history. For the next 14 months the site remained under the watchful eye of caretaker William McDonald of Deposit. In December 1936, Army officials sent McDonald home and prepared to dismantle the buildings, which were reportedly sold to area buyers.[19] One building was moved to Deposit High School for use as an athletic field storage structure.[20]

*The 1934 Annual Report to the Legislature by the NYS Conservation Dept. said the 421 men employed at 35 camps as project superintendents, foremen, blacksmiths, tractor operators and mechanics earned a monthly payroll of $54,269, most of it spent in the small towns nearest the camps.

CHAPTER 7

CAMPSITES FOR THE

CATSKILLS

TANNERSVILLE, CAMP S-97
GREENE COUNTY
MAY 15, 1934–
OCTOBER 10, 1937

I t was a hot and lazy Sunday in midsummer 1934. Hundreds of people had driven to North Lake in Haines Falls, Greene County, to check out progress at the "new" state campsite, picnic under the trees and cool off by the lake. Now, late in the afternoon, many had left their blankets and baskets to walk half a mile or more to enjoy commanding views of the Hudson River from ledges a thousand feet above the valley floor.

The peace of their Sunday idyll came to a crashing halt with the muted sounds of fire sirens from Haines Falls and Tannersville, followed by the bleating of automobile horns from down in the parking lot and shouts of warning from people running up the trails. Then, across the ridge drifted the smell of smoke, "and the real exodus began."

Hurrying back to the lake, visitors were met by "a fearsome sight ... a dirty yellow column of smoke 300 feet high boiled upward as if forced by some mighty blower. It marked the center of the oncoming fire," which was fast approaching the famed Catskill Mountain House and state-owned picnic grounds nearby.

Forest rangers ordered everyone out of the park, but headed in the opposite direction, toward the advancing flames, were truckloads of young men from the nearby Civilian Conservation Corps camp in Tannersville coming to the rescue.

"It was a joy to watch them swing into action," reported the *Stamford Mirror-Recorder* on July 26. "No sooner would a truck come to a stop than the entire outfit would pop out and boys with pumping outfits on their back would head for the lake for a supply of water, a camp foreman barking orders as they ran. There was neither loss of time or motion. Other trucks quickly brought more boys and other fighting equipment, axe squads, rake squads, etc. As fast as a CCC boy would empty his tank he would take it on the run for a new supply. The camp commander and its chaplain were among those donning 35-pound water tanks and attacking burning trees with axes.

"It was a hot day, and a hot job. Most of them were wearing sleeveless jerseys and the hot cinders punished them unmercifully until another truck brought a load of sweaters which were donned quickly, and then they went at the fire like bearcats."

CCC Camp S-97 had an idyllic location on a plateau at the base of Clum Hill and overlooking Rip Van Winkle Lake. This photo was taken in July 1934, just two months after Company 291 arrived. John Ham

Aided by a pumper from the local fire department, the CCC and other volunteers brought the fire under control by 10 PM. The first CCC crew went back to camp for some shut-eye. At 3 AM the men returned to relieve the second crew, according to a story on August 4 in the camp newspaper, the *Tannersville Tiger*.

Startling though it was for the picnickers forced to flee, the fire that swept through the forest on the edge of the legendary escarpment that summer Sunday was not unusual. Fires sparked by passing trains, lightning or carelessness had so often consumed large sections of woodland in this high-peaks area that, in 1909, the state erected a fire observation tower atop Hunter Mountain, one of the first three towers in the Catskills that went up that year.[1]

What was different about the fire in 1934 was the ready availability of 200 vigorous young men, trained in the use of Indian tanks (portable water tanks) and all too familiar with rakes, axes

This closer postcard view of the Tannersville CCC camp must have been taken in the summer of 1934, as some of the tents that were first erected when the camp was occupied in May of that year are visible at right. Lonnie Gale

and hoes. They were the members of CCC Company 291 who occupied Camp S-97 in Tannersville, dubbed Camp Rip Van Winkle after the small lake it overlooked.

The camp, established in May 1934, existed for three and a half years. Its enrollees built hiking trails and truck roads, planted trees, constructed dams and developed two campsites on lands the state had acquired in the late 1920s and early 1930s. One of those campsites was North Lake, where they'd been called on their day off to beat back the flames that July afternoon.

In 1930 the state had acquired 2,197 acres of wild and scenic mountain land that had once constituted the domain of the storied Catskill Mountain House. The hotel had been offering sublime views and gracious hospitality since its construction in 1824. In its heyday the Mountain House was a premiere destination for notable people who enjoyed the vista from its pillared portico, a familiar landmark for valley residents. Guests strolled around North and South Lakes, meandered on carriage roads, played tennis and croquet, carved their names in the rock ledges and captured the majesty of the site on sketch pad and canvas. But changing travel patterns and tourist tastes brought about the hotel's decline, and its owners in 1930 sold most of the surrounding property to the state for $12 an acre.[2]

While the Mountain House continued to operate on its smaller holdings through 1942, a more pedestrian crowd flocked to the new campsite the state was developing all around it. The CCC was put to work there as soon as they were settled into their tents in nearby Tannersville. "A large area along the shore of North Lake has already been cleared, trees have been thinned out, undergrowth removed, plots for camps leveled and top-dressed with shale, a large number of fireplaces have been constructed, a water system with outlets has been installed and the work is being extended into the forest," reported the *Mirror-Recorder* on July 26, 1934.

The CCC boys also built several latrines and a 10,000-gallon concrete reservoir. They equipped dozens of campsites with fireplaces and wood supplies, constructed a six-room house to replace a canvas-covered structure, and, with help from enrollees of Veterans CCC Camp S-119 from Livingstonville in Schoharie County, operating from a temporary tent camp between Hunter and Tannersville, built three miles of camp roadway. The lake was cleaned and an earthen dam constructed at the site of the old spillway to raise the water level by almost two feet.[3]

The area became an instant attraction. "The new park within a very few weeks has become tremendously popular," said the *Mirror-Recorder*. "With all the places prepared for picknickers, there was not one unused fireplace or picnic table available last Sunday afternoon."* And so the CCC, determined to protect the state's—and

---

*North Lake State Campground has remained every bit as popular in the seven decades since its construction. The state acquired thousands of additional acres (including the site of the Mountain House, which was intentionally burned in 1966) and eventually connected North and South Lakes.

Company 291, along with camp officers, work foremen and kitchen crew, posed with their canine mascot for this portrait in June 1936. Mountain Top Historical Society

its own—investment, came on the run when smoke was spotted, contributing to the 14,348 man-days committed by corps enrollees to fire suppression statewide in 1934.[4]

Company 291 next turned its attention to Devil's Tombstone State Campsite in a mountain notch known as Stony Clove. Named for a large upended boulder, the site was modestly developed in the 1920s on land the state had acquired in 1909.[5] In 1931 it included just half a dozen "fireplace campsites."[6]

Today called a "campground," Devil's Tombstone lies along State Route 214. It is situated in a dramatic gorge where the state added to its holdings by buying 1,500 acres in 1933. Until 1940, trains of the Stony Clove and Catskill Mountain Railroad carried passengers and freight through the gorge between Phoenicia in Ulster County and Hunter in Greene County. (The railroad's Tannersville station was a stone's throw from CCC Camp Rip Van Winkle.)[7]

"Carelessness caused the fire that destroyed this forest" declares the sign posted by the NYS Conservation Department on the ravaged side of Plateau Mountain in Stony Clove, Greene County, in 1919. Replanting such forests and preventing future blazes was a large part of the CCC's work in the 1930s. This photo was taken by Clinton G. Abbott, a noted conservationist who later directed the San Diego Natural History Museum for many years. NYS Archives

Capitalizing on the attractive setting and on the availability of CCC labor, the state not only added campsites and improved facilities at the campground, but also created the small lake that now serves as a landmark in the clove. Company 291 built the stone masonry dam across a wetland to impound the eight-acre lake. With Livingstonville veterans, they also built the half-mile road through the campground.[8]

The company had come to the Catskills with some hard-core experience wielding shovels and mattocks. Organized at Camp Dix, New Jersey, on May 18, 1933, Company 291 went first to Cascade, Idaho, where they spent six months planting trees and building fire trails, ranger cabins and observation towers in the National Forest, and building a suspension bridge across the Salmon River.

In October the company was relocated to Criglersville, Virginia, along the Skyline Drive that was then under construction. Company 291 worked mostly on road construction there.[9]

The company moved to Tannersville the following spring. An advance cadre set up an initial tent village on Clum Hill on May 14, 1934. The rest of the company arrived May 17. That summer, winter-worthy wooden barracks, a recreation hall, a mess hall and other buildings were constructed. At first the camp drew water from a spring. Later it was served by the Village of Tannersville municipal supply. Latrines were soon replaced by flush toilets connected to the local sewer system, which was owned and operated by New York City to protect water quality in its 10-year-old Schoharie Reservoir downstream.[10]

This beautiful aerial image shows North and South Lakes in Haines Falls, high above the Hudson Valley, where Camp S-97 helped develop a state campground that proved instantly popular. The Catskill Mountain House sits on the hilltop on the upper right.
NYS Archives

Truckin'

The truck trails built by Company 291 were part of a larger effort by the state to get mechanized equipment and trucks bearing firefighters to the scenes of forest fires more quickly.

Gasoline-operated fire pumps and specially equipped trucks were effective in stemming fire losses, if they could get there in a timely manner. During 1931 and 1932, the Conservation Department experimented with opening old turnpikes crossing private lands in the Catskills so they could accommodate trucks. They proved useful, but money and manpower shortages did not allow expansion of the idea—until the CCC was born.

The state identified 38 road projects totaling 116 miles in the Adirondack and Catskill Forest Preserves according to the degree of fire hazard in the area, its inaccessibility, how much land the state owned in the vicinity, and whether there were existing roads that could be reconstructed without cutting new ones through the Forest Preserve. Nine roads, measuring 27 miles in length, were approved in the Catskills.

In the summer of 1934, Company 291 reconstituted a 3.7-mile road from what is now Route 23A between Lexington and Hunter, over the back side of Colonel's Chair into the Spruceton Valley. The road crossed the saddle between 4,040-foot Hunter Mountain and 3,680-foot Rusk Mountain. The *Tannersville Tiger* newspaper of August 4, 1934, explained that work had begun at the Spruceton end. The road crossed Hunter Brook on a 22-foot bridge with wooden deck, stone abutments and steel girders, "the steel taken from the old water tower at the site of the old Kaaterskill House. Continuing on from Hunter Creek [officially Hunter *Brook*], the road will extend north-east for a distance of a mile and a quarter, rising nine hundred feet to the top of the mountain, where we swing nearly north and in a distance of two miles drop fifteen hundred feet to the Schoharie Creek.

"Even with hand labor, as ours must essentially be, we expect to be on top of the mountain with a good dirt road by September first. The principal use, of course, is to make the top of Hunter Mountain accessible in the event of a forest fire." In 1937 firefighters used the truck trail to reach and extinguish a 26-acre fire. Forest historian Michael Kudish described the territory around Hunter Mountain as "the interior fire capital of the Catskills," where at least six major forest fires have blackened the landscape since the mid-nineteenth century.

The Tannersville boys also reconstructed a 1.3-mile truck trail to provide access to Kaaterskill Mountain (Kaaterskill High Peak), which today serves as the beginning of the trail to Huckleberry Point.

Once a fire road was constructed in the Forest Preserve, it was barricaded so that unauthorized vehicles could not use it. During deer hunting season the Conservation Department arranged for local CCC camps to have two enrollees stationed at each barricade from 6 AM to

CCC boys guard a truck trail against access during hunting season by anything other than firefighting vehicles. NYS Archives

The Conservation Department's state-of-the-art firefighting truck, as shown in the department's 1937 Annual Report. The CCC did much of the backbreaking labor involved in reconstituting old logging roads to provide access by the new trucks to interior forest fires.

6 PM daily. Their job was to warn off anyone, other than those on foot, who attempted to pass the barricade, and to get the license numbers of those who resisted.

Truck trails were also built through reforested areas outside the Forest Preserve, but they could be used for administrative and recreation purposes as well as for firefighting access. Breakabeen Camp S-93 takes the record in that category, building 9.6 miles of road. More than half of that was finished in the camp's first summer of work, in 1934. Some of these roads, including a few in the Windham and Tannersville areas and in southern Schoharie County, are still known locally as "CCC Roads." Roads were built ten feet wide, with two-foot shoulders. Eight to ten inches of broken rock were used as a sub-base, topped with three to four inches of fine shale or gravel. John Jankowski of Amsterdam remembered using a sledge hammer to break up rock for those roads, "just like in the prison movies! But it was fun, because we were young."

Conservation Department Annual Reports for 1936, 1937 and 1940; memo from Conservation Dept. to District Rangers, Oct. 17, 1935; *The Catskill Forest: A History* (Michael Kudish); interview with John Jankowski, Nov. 23, 2007; *Tannersville Tiger,* Aug. 4, 1934

H. C. Folts, a captain in the Infantry Reserves, was an early commander of Camp S-97. His four-year-old son reportedly christened the camp using a bottle of water from Rip Van Winkle Lake, a ceremony that involved "a snake dance, war whoops with axes, buffoonery and clowning in the recreation hall at which enrollees and guests from Tannersville rocked in glee."[11]

A month after its arrival the company read in the *Tannersville Tiger* of the work plans that Camp Superintendent R. P. Pendorf had for them. They were to build two dams, one at North Lake, one in Stony Clove; a 3.5-mile truck trail between Hunter and Rusk Mountains; a foot trail from Stony Clove to the Hunter Mountain fire tower connecting with the truck trail and another from the village through Mossy Brook to the Colonel's Chair (the peak where Hunter Mountain Ski Bowl would be built in 1960).

Plans also called for building foot trails from Stony Clove over Plateau Mountain to Mink Hollow; from Elka Park to the top of

The "Devil's Tombstone" (boulder at right) gave its name to a state campsite developed by junior CCC men from Tannersville and by veterans from Livingstonville, Schoharie County, who occupied a temporary camp in Hunter. NYS Archives

The CCC dammed Stony Clove Creek (pictured) to create a lovely lake in this dramatic gorge near Devil's Tombstone Campsite (now Campground). NYS Archives

Mink Hollow notch; from Platte Clove over Indian Head, Twin and Sugar Loaf Mountains to Mink Hollow; and around North Lake. A two-mile telephone line would be strung from Stony Clove to the fire tower, and four lean-tos would also be constructed.

The North Lake Campsite project looked daunting: build 100 fireplaces, 150 tables, 2 bathhouses, 10 toilets and a beach, not to mention campsite roads and picnic ground improvements. But, reported the *Tiger* on June 23, 1934, "The boys have made a good start in our work. One mile of the Hunter Mountain road has been built, the trail to the top of Hunter Mountain is nearly finished, one and a half miles of the foot trail around North Lake has been constructed. On this trail, the boys have built a rustic foot bridge and considerable log walk bridging the wet spots. The old Kaaterskill Road has been opened up, and good progress has been made on enlargement of the North Lake campsite."

The youthful reporter joked that the blisters on their feet were beginning to disappear and "they have learned to slap punkies with one hand and shovel with the other." A visit on August 8, 1934, by Conservation Department Commissioner Lithgow Osborne and W. D. Mulholland, supervisor of recreational development for the State Conservation Department, was a great motivator. One young man, questioned by the officials as he attacked a stump with a mattock, "admitted that he had never worked harder in all his short life."

In the months to come, Company 291 also planted more than 800,000 deciduous trees and searched for gypsy moths and other pests on 5,500 acres across Windham, Halcott, Hunter, Jewett, Lexington and Prattsville. Eight miles of stream—on the West Kill, Hunter Creek and Batavia Kill—were improved to enhance fisheries.[12] Norman Van Valkenburgh recalls CCC men building stone-filled log cribbing on his father's farm on the West Kill when he was a boy. The sturdy docking is still there, he said in 2008.

The relationship between the camp and the community was apparently cordial and cooperative. Enrollees staged public boxing matches, took part in community theater (as in June 1934, when some were recruited for parts in *Henry's Wedding* put on by the local Knights of Pythias), and invited local youth to attend education classes at the camp. Offerings under Educational Advisor Murray Gillman included auto mechanics, physics, telephone and radio communication, photography and fingerprinting, as well as regular academic subjects. CCC athletes used the Tannersville High School ball field for games among themselves and with other area camps.[13]

The camp newspaper of August 4, 1934, reported that on July 23 the director of the Fairmont Hotel in Tannersville brought a troupe of performers to Rip Van Winkle Lake to entertain the company with skits and stand-up comedy. An orchestra played "Dinah," "Some of These Days," and the company theme, "Tiger Rag." Ball games were played against staffs at the Rose Garden Hotel, the Hillside and other local hotels, and Meyer's Candy Store once supplied "an ice cream supper" for the 200 enrollees.

At least one local boardinghouse didn't have much to do with the CCC. Charles Pappas and a partner had acquired a small Tannersville hotel in 1934 and ran it that summer as The Olympic, catering to a Greek clientele. Thirteen-year-old Matina Billias, Charles's niece, worked there with her sister and their mother, who kept a close eye on the girls. "I don't even remember seeing any of the CCC boys," related Matina, who years later met future husband George at another area boardinghouse. As a teenager, George had seen the long line at a CCC enrolling station in New York City and gave up the idea of joining. He did some work for the WPA instead and later sailed the seas as a merchant seaman. As retirees, George and Matina moved in 1976 to Tannersville to a house a block from Rip Van Winkle Lake, from which all traces of the CCC camp had disappeared.

Local and contract clergy performed religious services several times a month at the camp, and men also went into the village for Sunday Mass and other services. An Army doctor ministered to the enrollees' medical needs. While there were accidents (six reported in June 1936 alone), it seems to have been a pretty healthy place except for an occasional outbreak, like the "slight epidemic" of German measles that sickened 12 people in February 1935.[14]

The mess hall served stick-to-your-ribs fare like pancakes and sausage, spaghetti and meatballs, beef stew, meatloaf, baked beans and bread pudding. They were, after all, a hard-working crew, supervised by Chief Foreman W. E. Vroman. He was assisted by Foreman W. T. Riley, Blacksmith Patrick McDonough, Mechanic Harry Pastor, and Foremen William Mahon, Ralph Fancher, V. B. Hyatt, Peter Simpson, Frank Ulrich and others over the years. These were area men whose employment with Camp S-97 was good for them, and good for the local economy.[15]

Most of the initial enrollees in Company 291 hailed from the New York–New Jersey metropolitan region, but by 1936 its ranks had been augmented by transfers from Boiceville, when that camp closed, and included many local men from Haines Falls, Boiceville, Platte Clove, Tannersville, Elka Park, West Kill and Hensonville. Among the leaders who were paid a bit more for taking on additional responsibilities was William Reich of Tannersville.[16]

William was among six Brooklyn siblings whose mother was forced to put five of them in a Catholic orphanage when their father died and she could not care for them. Brothers William and

This campsite amphitheater at North Lake was created by the CCC working with the Conservation Department, which pictured the project in its 1938 Annual Report.

Joseph enrolled in the CCC when they came of age; William served at the Tannersville camp, Joseph in Livingstonville. William served in the Army during World War II, but otherwise spent most of his life in Tannersville. His son, William, recalls that his dad had such vivid memories of Camp Rip Van Winkle that he created a wooden model of it, which was on display for many years in the window of Warm's Restaurant in Tannersville. Joe Reich was a Tannersville village justice for many years.[17]

As at many other CCC camps, a few of the enrollees found love in the local community. Local historian Justine Hommel recalled as a young girl watching from the sidewalk captivated by the spectacle of her first wedding, at which the groom's CCC comrades created an arch of shovels for the newlyweds to pass beneath.

The Tannersville CCC Camp was closed in October 1937. Its legacy includes not only North Lake and Devil's Tombstone State Campgrounds, but its own Rip Van Winkle Lake, where the members of Company 291 created a beach that today is owned and maintained by the Village of Tannersville for the enjoyment of local residents and visitors. More grandiose plans for that area once included a casino and dance hall, a boat livery, and campsites. Community boosters also envisioned a ski trail on Clum Hill (see "Ski Fever"). Some improvements were made over the years, but the lake and environs remained a modest park.

In 2008 the area is the focus of renewed attention. The village, with state grant funds, is planning to rejuvenate the park with a playground and other amenities, while a proposal to create a 100-lot subdivision encompassing the former "CCC lot" is being reviewed by local and regional officials.

CHAPTER 8

"IT WAS SURPRISING
WHAT THEY WOULD TAKE"

BREAKABEEN, CAMP S-93
SCHOHARIE COUNTY
MAY 18, 1935–
JANUARY 15, 1942

The longest-lived CCC camp in the Catskill region, and one of the most productive, was the reforestation camp near the hamlet of Breakabeen in the Town of Fulton, Schoharie County.

It was occupied by Company 222 in May 1934, at about the same time the Tannersville camp was being established. Before the Breakabeen camp closed in 1941, hundreds of young men had bunked in its barracks and toiled in field and forest, planting more than eight million trees, building nine miles of truck trails, erecting a fire tower and enhancing seven miles of streams to improve trout habitat. At least three enrollees were cited for brave rescues, including two who guided a family of eight from their home through the swirling floodwaters of Panther Creek in 1938, when their own camp was radically rearranged by the disaster.

In fact, Panther Creek was in a foul mood when a 16-man cadre from Company 222 first arrived on May 18, 1934, to unload supplies in advance of the arrival of the rest of the unit from its winter assignment in Chicopee, Massachusetts. They were greeted by rain and the sight of the creek rising at the edge of their campsite. Harry Goldstein remembered waking in his tent the next morning "just in time to see my suitcase and barracks bag floating the general direction of the Schoharie Creek." [1]

Even after the site dried out, it didn't present an appealing prospect to the campers. "The valley in which their new home was to be built was very rocky and covered by dense growth of brush," related a local newspaper on October 4, 1934. "They realized at once there would be plenty of hard work ahead but all pitched in and went to work with undaunted spirit."

More than 60 men lived in tents for the first few months until wooden barracks were completed in September. The site had been leased by the government for a dollar a year from owner Percy Partridge. Camp administrators, led by Captain David Kirk, commanding officer, occupied an old house on the property, which had once been the David Hilts farm.[2]

In fairly short order the 15-acre site on Bouck's Falls Road, about a half mile off NYS Route 30 and a few miles south of Middleburgh, included five 40-man bunkhouses, a bathhouse with 12 showers and several chemical toilets, a fireplace-equipped recreation hall with a stage, a library and a store, an education building,

CCC Camp S-93 was located on Bouck's Falls Road along Panther Creek in the Town of Fulton, between Breakabeen and Middleburgh. Ruth Dietz

Stream Work

All fish are not created equal.

The state devoted much of its efforts in the 1930s to making streams more livable for trout, a premiere game fish that paid for itself, then as now, in dollars brought in by anglers anxious to land a brookie or a rainbow in pristine waters.

A stream development program begun in 1934 targeted for improvement 187 miles of waterway on state lands or in reforestation areas, and, after 1935, streams where public fishing easements had been acquired. The CCC was called in to clear fallen timber and other debris from streams. To improve trout habitat, they built V-shaped dams to create pools and deflectors to increase stream velocity and create riffles. To control erosion they built log cribbing along stream banks.

The Bureau of Biological Survey of the Conservation Department's Division of Fish & Game supervised the projects. Masonville CCC enrollees working along Steam Mill and Oquaga Brooks planted willow cuttings in an experiment that found that the fast-growing cuttings provided stream-bank stability and shade required for optimum trout survival.

The Beaverkill and Willowemoc benefited from bank cribbing, log deflectors and channel blockers. On the West Kill, structures addressed "a very serious clay slide and gravel bar situation. This will return one-half mile of formerly unsatisfactory stream to trout production," according to the department's 1939 Annual Report. About 100 landowners along the West Kill and on the main stem of the Schoharie Creek donated fishing rights to the streams running through their lands in exchange for stream improvements, including a barrier dam on the Schoharie Creek near Prattsville to prevent coarse fish from ascending into trout waters.

A side camp of about 50 enrollees from Breakabeen Camp S-93 built the barrier in 1938 to keep black, or smallmouth, bass from migrating up the creek from the Schoharie Reservoir, which had

A temporary camp of about 50 enrollees from Breakabeen Camp S-93 built this barrier in 1938 to keep black, or smallmouth, bass from migrating up the creek from the Schoharie Reservoir. Diane Galusha

engulfed a waterfall that had served as a natural barrier to upstream migration. The bass had outgrown their food supply and had displaced the trout, so in the mid-1930s the Conservation Department relocated 1,000 undersized smallmouth bass from the creek above the reservoir to larger and warmer bodies of water. The success of that experiment prompted a more permanent measure, the construction of the barrier dam, which remains in place today.

The Breakabeen CCC workers also labored on Keyserkill, Betty Brook, Clapper Hollow and Cole Hollow streams.

"Move Bass from Schoharie Creek," *Oneonta Daily Star*, undated; "Breakabeen CCC Camp Observes 1st Anniversary," unidentified 1935 newspaper; Conservation Department Annual Reports 1936, 1939, 1940; *A Biological Survey of the Delaware & Susquehanna Watersheds 1935*; "CCC Boys Protect Schoharie Trout," *Catskill Mountain News*, June 10, 1938; *Land Acquisition for New York State, An Historical Perspective*, Norman Van Valkenburgh, 1985 an infirmary, quarters for Army officers and foresters, a 15-stall garage, a tool house and a blacksmith shop reportedly built around a large tree stump on which was mounted an anvil.[3]

Once the company was up to strength and settled, it began working on a long list of projects outlined by District Forester Milton Hick and overseen by camp work Supervisor Earl Brockway. Its first task was to plant more than a million trees in its environs and in neighboring Greene and Delaware Counties.[4]

First, "Noxious growth of sumac, soft maple, pin cherry, brush and other valueless vegetation" was cleared from the abandoned farmland to be planted.[5] An unidentified CCC enrollee, quoted in the *Schenectady Gazette*, explained, "We plant in squares, each tree six feet from the next. We may plant white pine, or mix it with red pine, Scotch pine, Norway or white spruce, European larch, black locust or white ash. After planting an area we make a 14-foot fire break by plowing and discing. It's disced yearly thereafter to keep fire from spreading to the planted area. Next we locate a spring, open it to 16 or 20 feet in diameter, and shore it up with brick as a further source of fire protection. There will be an average of six water holes to each thousand acres."[6]

Breakabeen enrollee John Jankowski said barbed wire fencing was strung around the water holes. (By 1936 they'd already built 22 of them.) Miles of fencing were also erected to keep grazing livestock and deer from dining on the newly planted stock. In winter, existing forest was thinned and pruned, and fire lanes were cleared. The resulting piles of limbs and trunks were made available to area residents for firewood.

Fourteen Breakabeen CCC men under Foreman "Pop" Van-DerBogart planted 18,300 red pine seedlings in one day in the fall of 1935. That's 50 trees every 60 seconds. The seedlings were planted in Summit, Schoharie County, according to the camp's own newspaper, *The Advance.*

Earth Work

Saving the soil was the focus of Camp SCS-5 in Gallupville, Schoharie County, one of only 12 CCC camps in the state whose work was directed by experts from the federal Soil Conservation Service (SCS).

Company 1286 arrived at the camp on Fox Creek in October 1935, many of them having been transferred from service in Clarkia, Idaho. They soon set to work on farms whose owners had signed agreements with the SCS to allow projects on their overworked fields.

"Here the land has been sowed in the same crops year after year, without thought that certain elements, hard to replace, were being taken out of the land by the greedy roots of growing greenery," explained a writer for the *Knickerbocker Press* on August 16, 1936. "Too many farmers, busy with the thousand and one routine chores of their industry, let ditches run where they might, chopped trees where earth needed roots to hold it in place, saw gullies reduce their tillable acreage because they didn't know what to do about it.

"In an earlier generation, the SCS might have found it difficult to coax farmers into letting it step in and correct such evils. The SCS would have been accused of interfering with the hand of God. Farmers of today, through recent setbacks, have been persuaded that God indeed helps those who help themselves."

Such help from the CCC over the next five years included digging diversion ditches, building check dams, seeding and sodding ditches, planting windbreaks and improving woodlands. They fenced off woodlots from grazing animals, and laid out fields for strip cropping and rotation planting.

Under the direction of a senior foreman named Ellis, Company 1286 built a kiln on Middle Road, near the camp, where there was an abundance of limestone. There they quarried more than 500 tons of stone and burned it to produce lime for fertilizing farm fields. "I used to draw lime from there for our fields," recalled Robert Loden in 1999.

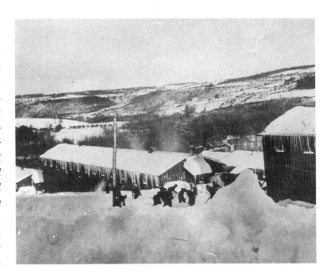

CCC members at Gallupville, the only soil conservation camp in the region, were called upon to remove snow from their camp roads and sidewalks as well as curb erosion and fertilize Schoharie farmlands. Schoharie County Historical Society, Chet Zimmer Collection

His family farm adjoined the camp, and the CCC, including brother Al Loden, worked there, "taking out stone walls, and making fields larger. The men worked in our woodland, taking out brush and decaying trees. They did a good job building ponds and dikes along Fox Creek."

The Gallupville CCC also planted 90,000 trees around the Altamont Reservoir to prevent erosion and provide natural filtration to protect water quality. They planted another 12,000 pines and spruce on the hillside behind Cobleskill High School.

The boys of Company 1286 were credited with stopping a house fire in Gallupville in February 1936, and with saving horses from a burning barn on another occasion. "As a result, a number of the CCC boys became guests in local homes and entered into the life of the townspeople," recalled former company member Robert Egan.

Camp SCS-5 operated through at least 1940. Some of its buildings still stand, occupied as residences.

Knickerbocker News, Dec. 22, 1935, Aug. 16, 1936; *Schoharie Republican,* Feb. 27, 1936, April 1, 1937, and undated 1940 articles; *Altamont Enterprise,* July 15, 1999; *The Conservationist,* Nov.–Dec. 1986; *Schenectady District CCC Yearbook for 1936*

"I had a lot of respect for the boys," said Supervisor Earl Brockway in a 1996 interview for *Ulster Magazine*. "It was a lot of hard, manual labor. A lot of blisters on their hands. If a guy goldbricked, lay down on the job, the other boys got on him. When the temperature was zero we took 'em. When it was below, we didn't. ... It was surprising what they would take."[7]

During their first year afield, Breakabeen boys were trucked to Stamford, Delaware County, to build a 68-foot fire tower on Mt. Utsayantha, where several wooden observation towers had been blown down by high winds over the years. The state acquired the new steel tower and engaged the CCC to erect it on the mountaintop, which had been willed to the Village of Stamford. It did not take long for the tower to prove its worth, as the resident fire spotter reported 15 forest fires in 1935. Also in 1934, Breakabeen CCC workers constructed the base of a fire tower on Hooker Hill in the Town of Maryland, Otsego County. The Stamford and Hooker Hill observers worked in tandem to triangulate fire locations. [8]

Many Breakabeen enrollees came from the Schenectady-Amsterdam area. John Jankowski, tired of waiting in line day after day at carpet factories for jobs that did not materialize, went to Amsterdam City Hall with a group of friends to sign up for the CCC in the fall of 1935. "We'd get up at 6 AM when the bugle played and everyone got out of the barracks to raise the flag, just like in the Army," he recalled in 2007. The work was hard, but the food was okay ("They'd bring hot chocolate in milk cans to where we were working in the woods"), and there was fun, too. "We'd go to dances in Middleburgh, and we used to play cards, using matches for money."[9]

Donald Dietz joined the CCC in 1935, soon after graduating from Schoharie Central School. With no job and no money for college to follow his interest in journalism, Dietz dreamed instead of adventure at a CCC camp somewhere in the wild Rockies. "What I got was a 12-mile ride in a truck to Breakabeen," he recalled in a 1990 memoir. After a three-month stint in the woods, he was appointed as an assistant leader working with the camp's education director. Dietz helped organize and teach vocational and academic classes and, using his experience as editor of his high-school newspaper, launched a camp newspaper, *The Advance*. The monthly paper was professionally printed at the *Schoharie Republican* newspaper plant. Before his 16-month enrollment ended, Dietz also spent six months as assistant in the infirmary, "dispensing pills under the supervision of Dr. [Duncan] Best, bandaging cuts and occasionally helping clear up a black eye."[10]

Michael "Dutch" Irving was another assistant leader in the camp. Born in 1915, he worked in a grocery store to help support his parents and

Meal time was highly anticipated at the Breakabeen camp. These men are lined up at the mess hall door.

Ruth Dietz

Breakabeen CCC enrollees helped build this 68-foot steel fire tower at Mt. Utsayantha in Stamford, Delaware County, where tourists came by the busload to enjoy the view. Stamford Village Library

*Dr. Duncan Best
of Middleburgh
tended to sick
and injured CCC
enrollees at
Breakabeen.*
Best House

seven siblings who shared a cold-water flat in Harlem. He joined
the CCC in October 1933, serving at Fort Slocum on Long Island
before being sent to Breakabeen. A younger brother, Tom, also
spent time at Camp S-93.[11]

A middleweight boxer who reached the quarterfinals of the
New York City Golden Gloves in 1932, Irving trained fellow enrollees and competed in inter-camp matches, winning the Gloves title
in the 160-pound class in Albany in 1937. "Some of the guys who
came to camp from New York City thought they were tough, but
they were only tough in a group," he recalled in a 1983 interview.
"If a bunch of guys were giving me trouble, I'd pick out the big-
gest one and say, 'c'mon, let's have a little exhibition.' I'd blow the
whistle and the whole camp would come around to watch."[12]

Not surprisingly, Irving gained the respect of his fellows and
was named "top kick" in charge of temporary camps that were set

up at Prattsville, Greene County (see "Stream Work") and at Delmar, Albany County, where a detachment of about 50 men built a footbridge and two earthen dams at an experimental game farm raising grouse and wildfowl. (It later became the state's Five Rivers Environmental Education Center.)[13]

Some of the fighting done by enrollees was unauthorized, however. In December 1934, Assistant Leader Arthur Merkley, a 23-year-old from Buffalo, and Breakabeen resident Leo Bouck, 19, were involved in a brawl following a dance at the Baker House in Middleburgh. A 29-year-old Broome farmer, Walter Rozea, died as a result of the fray. Merkley and Bouck were indicted for manslaughter, but were found not guilty after a three-day trial in 1935.[14]

But there were tales of heroism among enrollees, too. In August 1934, Seymour Haas, with a discharged CCC member, Walter Parsons, saved a life. They found Flora Broadrick of Port Washington unconscious in her vehicle, which had slammed into a pole near camp. They pulled her from the wreckage and got her to a doctor. James Galtieri, a leader at S-93, was awarded the CCC Certificate of Valor by Director Robert Fechner after he allowed himself to be lowered by a rope 200 feet down a cliff face to rescue a fellow enrollee suffering from exhaustion.[15]

At the camp's fifth anniversary celebration in May 1939, Louis Sargent of Schenectady and Michael Hogan of Maspeth were also presented with the CCC Certificate of Valor for saving the Bouck family, which had been stranded by floodwaters in their home near the CCC camp. The pair, assisted by other enrollees, improvised a lifeline in the dark to guide seven adults and an infant from the home "surrounded by approximately 800 feet of swift raging water filled with debris."[16] The flood caused extensive damage to roads, bridges and buildings in the region, and knocked several camp buildings off their foundations. It took weeks to put things back together.[17]

Fire!

As they coaxed new forests to life and built observation towers, stone-lined water ponds and fire breaks to protect them, CCC enrollees also knocked down fires that threatened new plantations.

Company 222 at Breakabeen was called out to fight three fires in two days during the fall of 1935. Hunters were blamed for charring five acres near Grand Gorge on October 20. An out-of-control brush fire burned two acres near Fultonham the following day, and that evening 42 men jammed into a truck for a ride to Cole Hollow. There, a two-acre blaze required "hard work on a steep ravine in pitch darkness."

Fire protection in New York State was organized by Fire Towns (communities located in the Adirondack and Catskill Forest Preserves) and Fire Districts (important forest areas outside the Preserves). Fire Towns represented an area of 7.5 million acres of land "of which 80 percent comprises the most valuable forests of the state," according to the Conservation Department's 1939 Annual Report. Fire Districts made up a greater amount of land (9.5 million acres), but they were only 45 percent forested.

The state's protection and firefighting efforts had necessarily been concentrated in the Fire Towns, but the availability of the CCC allowed much more work to be done in the districts during the 1930s.

Laurens CCC enrollees are pictured dousing a brush fire.
NYS CCC Museum

The CCC built countless stone-lined ponds in reforestation areas to serve as reservoirs for firefighting purposes. 1938 NYS Conservation Department Annual Report

Later that same decade, however, technological developments ultimately reshaped fire spotting and made obsolete the towers the CCC had erected and the telephone lines they had strung over forested hill and dale.

The Conservation Department's 1937 Annual Report declared that radio equipment would likely never supplant telephones as the primary communication means from tower observers to rangers and firefighters. But just two years later radio "was beyond the preliminary experimental stage," and that year it "efficiently aided both the detection and suppression of forest fires in the southern Catskill region and throughout Orange and Sullivan Counties."

Radio-equipped trucks and a new weapon in the war against forest fires—airplanes—were in general use by the early 1940s.

Those advances notwithstanding, dozens of towers and more than 400 miles of telephone line continued to be used for the next two or three decades. Nor have the tools used to extinguish fires on fields and mountainsides changed much since 1934, when the department purchased the following: 6 gasoline operated pumps; 22,000 feet of hose; 600 knapsack pumps; 90 crated tool outfits, each consisting of 2 knapsack pumps, 2 shovels, 2 brooms, 2 fire rakes, an axe and 6 canvas pails.

Conservation Department Annual Reports, 1934–42; *The Advance*, October 1935

This sign warned hunters that CCC workers were in the woods.
Diane Galusha

Indeed, the camp had its ups and downs. For the first two years, the company's work accomplishments, enrollment, attendance records and camp morale were at high levels. In 1935 it earned a medal from the War Department for being one of the outstanding camps in the eastern United States. But a change in command in 1937, and the enrollment of some less than savory characters, resulted in many desertions and dishonorable discharges (38 in the 12 months ending in June 1938). Accusations of misfeasance, ineptitude and abuse were leveled by and against camp leaders, and S-93 captured the unwelcome attention of CCC administrators at the highest level. But a change in Army commanders and a bit of house cleaning reversed the decline, so that the camp, which had sunk to the lowest ranking in its district, was again number one by 1939.[18]

The turnaround was reflected in the camp's first-place finish in the 4th Annual Sub-District Track and Field Meet held at Middleburgh High School on October 1, 1938. Red Gehring of Breakabeen high-jumped 5 feet 9 inches, besting by six inches the record set the previous year by a Margaretville leaper. Competitors from those two camps, as well as from Livingstonville, Altamont and Gallupville, were awarded medals and trophies at a banquet following the meet.[19]

As at all other CCC camps, the Breakabeen facility offered wide-ranging educational and recreational programs. The October 1935 *Advance*, for example, contained announcements that basketball and debate teams were organizing, that 18 pairs of skis had been acquired for races and touring, and that drama, music, mechanics and electricity courses had been added. There were weekly movies and an active library, which by 1940 had 800 books, 7 newspapers and several magazines.

A 1939 camp inspection report showed classes offered in such topics as spelling, surveying, carpentry, current events, typing and map reading. "We have had a number of boys go out from this camp and secure

Bertha and Madison Hilts acquired the Breakabeen camp and used the buildings as a tourist destination called Madison Garden Village. Most of the buildings survived multiple ownership and uses, and today many, including the infirmary (pictured above), are occupied as residences.

Phil Skowfoe (left) Diane Galusha, (above)

positions," reported William Furlong, Education Advisor. "Skilled workmen were not turned out, but boys did know enough about the work to give them a start in a trade."[20]

While many enrollees left Company 222 to take jobs in the improving economy, others stepped from the CCC uniform into Army fatigues. Enrollment in the Breakabeen camp was down to just 69 by October 1941. The camp closed for good January 15, 1942.

The accomplishments of Company 222 in the seven years spent at Camp 93 can be itemized in statistics that have little meaning to those who have never wielded a mattock or a chain saw, or spent hours stumbling over rocky, log-strewn hillsides in all kinds of weather: 8 million trees planted, 45 miles of fire break dug, 1,200 rods of fencing strung, 80 water holes built, 9 miles of truck trails constructed, 3,200 acres of forest improved, 16,000 acres examined for white pine blister rust carriers, 5 miles of stream developed, 950 acres of forest hazard reduction, 75 miles of surveys completed.[21]

The camp's greater legacy may lie in the human potential such work uncovered. "President Roosevelt did a good thing," says former CCC worker John Jankowski. "The CCC got boys off the streets and helped them develop."[22]

CHAPTER 9
WORKING HARD SO
OTHERS COULD PLAY

MARGARETVILLE, CAMP S-133
DELAWARE COUNTY
OCTOBER 26, 1935–
OCTOBER 22, 1938

t was the middle of the Great Depression.

Lou Kole was a 15-year-old kid looking for a way out of Jamaica, Long Island where his father "worked on and off" to support his family of five. Lou lied about his age, signed up for the Civilian Conservation Corps, then borrowed two cents from a fellow enrollee to send his folks a postcard from the Fort Dix training center, telling them what he'd done and not to worry.

Hank Geary was also 15, living in a Catholic orphanage in Nanuet. One day he and two other boys decided they "didn't want to stay there anymore" and ran off to the CCC enrollment center, convincing authorities they were 18.

Robert Barnes was the second-oldest of 13 children on the family farm near Downsville. "Crowded out of the nest," the 17-year-old walked 20 miles from the Barnes' Gregory Hollow homestead to enroll in the CCC at its Margaretville camp.

Their backgrounds were different, but hard times had pushed them in the same direction—to the CCC's Camp Delaware, a half mile south of the Village of Margaretville in Delaware County. The experience would change their young lives and leave an imprint on each of them that lasted into old age.

Over three years, from October 1935 to October 1938, Kole, Geary, Barnes and hundreds of other youths left their own mark on the Catskill forest, carving ski trails and hiking paths, building campsites and lean-tos, restoring stream banks and planting hundreds of thousands of trees in plantations that still bear witness to their efforts.

The first contingent of 125 enrollees from Company 1230 arrived in four special cars at the Margaretville station of the Delaware & Northern Railroad on October 26, 1935. Trucks took them from the station to the camp on a plateau overlooking the East Branch of the Delaware River. The campus of 14 buildings, including five barracks, each 115 feet long and 20 feet wide, had been constructed from prefabricated panels shipped from Mississippi. The camp was among the first to use the new, faster construction method that replaced the stick-built style of earlier camps. Panels and other materials were hauled from the railroad siding to the site by Margaretville hardware store owner Morgan Garrison, who received 65¢ a ton for the service.[1]

Members of Company 1230 helped build some of the structures at Camp Delaware in Margaretville. Joseph Monteleone

The Margaretville camp was situated on five acres of farmland leased to the government by Roy Leonard. It was built by a crew of about 50 local laborers and tradesmen under the supervision of Army Lt. George Drum, who lived at the home of Margaretville dentist Dr. James Gladstone while the facility was being built. Camp 133 included a mess hall to accommodate 200 men, a recreation hall, an eight-bed infirmary, quarters for Army officers and resident foresters, an office, storage buildings, and garages for a dozen Army and forestry trucks. Water for flush toilets and a washhouse was pumped from a 110-foot well to a 2,000-gallon storage tank erected on a knoll on the property. Sewage went to a septic tank and leach field.[2]

A flagpole, streets lined with whitewashed cobblestone, and landscaping were added by the first group of enrollees at Camp Delaware. But they soon discovered that a long list of other projects had been proposed for them to tackle. District Forest Ranger Leon Furch, interviewed by the *Catskill Mountain News* four months before the company arrived, enumerated some of the tasks he had in mind for the boys:

Camp S-133 perched on the side of a hill overlooking the East Branch of the Delaware River near the Village of Margaretville. Joseph Monteleone

- A telephone line from the Balsam Lake fire tower to Hanley Corners (nine miles), and a truck road from that tower to the Beaverkill (two miles). The tower itself had been erected by the state in 1931 to replace an older one.
- A truck road from Route 17 to the Twadell Point fire tower near East Branch.
- Conversion of a former state fish hatchery near Margaretville to a forest ranger headquarters.
- Construction of a public campground in the East Branch Valley (Beaverkill State Campground).
- A foot trail from Millbrook Road to the Balsam Lake tower, and a hiking/ski trail from Margaretville to Furlough Lake along Dry Brook Ridge.
- Forest improvement and planting on 1,100 acres.
- Forest pest control on 166,000 acres in the Towns of Middletown and Colchester.

All this and other jobs would take 137,950 man-days, Furch estimated. There was no shortage of work to be done in the 35- to 40-mile radius that was the camp's work zone.[3]

They started in November by trimming brush and dead trees along Cat Hollow Road. In December they began grading slopes at a new ski center near Phoenicia (see "Ski Fever"). Their numbers were bolstered by a contingent of 38 men who somehow managed to escape injury when the truck bringing them to camp from Newark overturned on the icy road near Highland, according to the *Kingston Freeman* of January 4, 1936. Soon after, another 42 enrollees from the closed Boiceville camp brought the company up to full strength, and they began transforming a former fish hatchery into a regional headquarters for State Forest Rangers.

The Delaware Fish Hatchery had opened in 1902 but closed in 1933 when the waters of Whortleberry Brook used at the hatchery

It's not clear how the "Suicide Gang" got its name, but they had their own banner and flew it proudly at this worksite. Joseph Monteleone

were deemed too cold to raise brook trout to adequate size for stocking. The state still owned the property on Huckleberry Brook Road across the valley from the CCC camp. It included a barn, a caretaker's house and smaller buildings once devoted to hatchery operations. The CCC boys demolished the barn and an icehouse, built a new storehouse and garage, and renovated the residence. Rock walls were built along the brook, and the surrounding plantation of Norway spruce was trimmed and thinned.[4] The project was completed in 1938.[5]

However, because District Ranger Furch already had a house in Fleischmanns, where district administrative offices were located, the Huckleberry Brook headquarters was not occupied until 1946, when Ranger Lester Rosa moved in and forest firefighting equipment was moved there from Fleischmanns. Seven years later Rosa moved his family to a new home near Arkville, and a reorganization of the Conservation Department split operations for this area between Oneonta and the City of Middletown. The Huckleberry Brook house then was sold by the state to a local family, which had it physically relocated to a homesite on a mountainside nearby. The NYS Department of Environmental Conservation still uses the rest of the property for storage.[6]

Another project attempted to capitalize on the growing skiing craze. The state put the CCC members to work building a 16-foot-wide ski trail from Margaretville along the crest of Pakatakan Mountain and Dry Brook Ridge to Mill Brook Road to connect with the Balsam Lake Mountain trail. Reported the *Catskill Mountain News* on April 3, 1936, "This when completed will give the skiing public an eight- or nine-mile trail affording the expert as well as the novice skier ample opportunity to demonstrate his skill."

Leonard Monteleone, a Brooklynite whose nickname was "Bullhead," was on the crew that worked on that trail until it became apparent that getting to the trailhead and hiking several miles in and out of the woods didn't leave much time for actual work.

After a hard day's work it was time to do the laundry and read the paper in this Margaretville barracks. Joseph Monteleone

The Trickle-Down Theory

Company 1230 was initially commanded by Captain D. G. Paston, who was heartily welcomed at a dinner he threw for local officials and social welfare administrators soon after the group arrived in Margaretville. Area boosters considered the camp a boon at a time when business was bad. They eagerly anticipated monthly paychecks to the enrollees and to the "Local Experienced Men" (LEMs), who could be counted on to spend some of that money in taverns and stores in the vicinity. And they welcomed the infusion of government funds for perishable food and other supplies purchased locally.

"The Civilian Conservation Corps has proven to be a very efficient agency for the stimulation of business," according to the 1935 Annual Report to the Legislature by the NYS Conservation Department. That year, 616 men were employed in 61 camps as superintendents, foremen, blacksmiths, tractor operators and mechanics. They earned a total of $85,000 a month. From May 1933 to October 1, 1935, civilian employees in New York State camps were paid nearly $1.3 million. With supplies, materials, equipment, transportation and utilities, expenditures in the state totaled $2,222,398. Much of that circulated through the communities hosting CCC camps.

In late 1935, as the federal government contemplated eliminating hundreds of CCC camps nationwide to cut spending, the impact of the enrollees' paychecks on their families was an important consideration. CCC Director Robert Fechner calculated that corps members had contributed $240 million to date to needy dependents back home. Margaretville enrollee Michael Strada said the $25 from his $30 paycheck that was sent home to his folks every month went a long way toward paying the family's $29 rent bill.

Conservation Dept. Annual Report 1935; *Catskill Mountain News*, Nov. 1, 1935; 2004 interviews with Michael Strada

It's hard to say what's in the bottle, but this group of Margaretville CCC men appears in a celebratory mood. Joseph Monteleone

Since they maintained a strict eight-hour-a-day work schedule, the ski trail project was abandoned. For reasons unknown, Leonard called the trail crew "The Suicide Gang," his son Joe recalls. The elder Monteleone joined the CCC when it began in 1933. He worked in Black Forks, Utah, High Point State Park in New Jersey, and in Bedford, Virginia, before coming to Margaretville, where in 1936 he was an assistant leader. In order to stay in the CCC after his enrollment period was up, he re-enrolled, using his brother Jack's name.

"He was really adept with an axe and a shovel, and he had to have learned that in the CCC," said Joe Monteleone. Years later, vacationing in the Catskills that he remembered so fondly, Leonard looked up his CCC foreman, Jim Minnerly, in Roxbury. In 1958 he bought Minnerly's hunting camp with another Margaretville CCC worker, Mike Mauceri. Their families enjoyed the property for decades, and still do.

In the spring of 1936, it looked like the fickle winds emanating from Washington might blow Company 1230 to Texas and close the Margaretville camp. But the storm passed and the work went on.[7]

In June 1936, a temporary tent camp of 45 men from Margaretville was set up not far from Livingston Manor to develop Beaverkill State Campsite.[8] The state had purchased former farmland in 1927 and 1928 from Margaret Ackerly, Frederich Keays and Frank and Nettie Kinch.[9] The Conservation Department established simple campsites there along the Beaverkill, a famous trout stream that is a tributary of the East Branch of the Delaware River. The facility first welcomed visitors in the summer of 1928, and in 1929 a ranger was stationed there. He supervised its operations, along with Woodland Valley and Devil's Tombstone campsites, which had been established in 1926.[10] (Company 1230 also helped improve Woodland Valley. See "The Campground at the End of the Road.")

In 1931 the site consisted of ten fireplaces, "a large camp-site" and bathhouses near "a deep, natural pool close to the old and picturesque covered bridge which spans the [Beaverkill] stream."[11] Expansion plans called for 30 individual campsites with fireplaces and tables to be built, as well as two sets of latrines and a picnic area with 15 fireplaces and tables. A reservoir was to be constructed and 3,000 feet of piping laid.[12] The seasonal work camp was reoccupied annually until the project was completed by the company after its move to Masonville (see Chapter 10).

In a 2004 interview, Michael Strada recalled working at the Beaverkill. "We built the road from the bridge along the river to the campsites. We built the fireplaces—experienced masons found the rocks and cut them up, we helped do the concrete. Campers came in with pup tents," he added. "We had our eyes on their daughters."

A narrow, twisting road known locally as the "Barkaboom" led from Margaretville to the Beaverkill work area. It was a challenge for unfamiliar drivers. Strada and other former CCC workers recalled an enrollee from Georgia driving into a ravine, killing himself and a local girl he was dating. On September 5, 1936, a CCC truck loaded with nine boys returning to the side camp from a night out in Liberty sideswiped a car carrying a New Jersey couple and injured the passenger.[13]

Leonard Monteleone, who took many photos of life at the Margaretville camp, posed for his own portrait with a CCC truck. Joseph Monteleone

Michael Strada on his way to the bathhouse at CCC Camp 133 and, almost 70 years later, visiting the site of the camp where he spent a memorable part of his young life.
Michael Strada; Diane Galusha

In August 1936, the company was called to help fight a large forest fire in the Accord area of Ulster County. It took five days to douse the blaze. A Kerhonkson enrollee, Joseph Vilenius, was credited with directing a group of fellow enrollees to safety from a danger zone.[14] Michael Strada remembers getting lost while fighting a fire. "It got dark and we stumbled on a group of men who'd also been fighting the fire. They'd killed a porcupine and were cooking it like a chicken over an open fire. I tried some, and I chewed and chewed. It got really cold that night. The next day they sent some people to rescue us." In its October 2, 1938, issue the *Catskill Mountain News* reported that CCC men and other volunteers fought a fire that burned 50 acres on the Milford Butler farm near Shavertown and another 50 acres of adjacent state land.

Young men who spent any time at all in the CCC learned valuable skills from capable practitioners known as "Local Experienced Men," or LEMs. Robert Barnes enjoyed working with Walton stonecutter Pop Fairchild. Lou Kole built Huckleberry Brook, Fox Hollow and Rider Hollow lean-tos with Jim Minnerly. Stanton Hogan, a Greene County enrollee, watched blacksmith Irving Trowbridge from Kelly Corners sharpen mattocks and spades on his forge and anvil. He also learned to drive a truck, which became his occupation. Seager Fairbairn learned the mechanic's art from Trowbridge and from Art Hill, a master mechanic who'd worked on airplanes in World War I and on automobiles at local car dealerships. Fairbairn would, in his own time, gain a fair amount of acclaim as a mechanical wizard and woodworker.

Robert Donahue, on the other hand, took to the clerical end of things. The Horseheads youth had spent some time at a CCC camp in VanEtten, New York, before being transferred to Margaretville in June 1937. "That was a wonderful summer for me," he

"Little Sampson" performed feats of strength in a performance for CCC men at Margaretville. Michael Strada

recalled in 2004. "I made a lot of friends. I worked on a dynamite crew, blasting holes in rock for the poles for the telephone line to Balsam Lake fire tower. I supervised seven or eight guys on a blister rust crew, pulling gooseberry bushes in an area now under the Pepacton Reservoir." In the fall he began helping with paperwork

Among the projects accomplished by Camp 113 was transforming a former state fish hatchery in Huckleberry Brook near Margaretville into a Conservation Department headquarters, which was occupied in the 1940s by Forest Ranger Lester Rosa, pictured at the site in 2004. Stanton Hogan

in the forestry office, and then got a civil service job with the Soil Conservation Service. After a three-year stint as company clerk and supply sergeant in World War II, Donahue pursued a career in New York State administration, retiring in 1976.

Hank Geary, the orphan from Nanuet, admits that he wasn't fond of Margaretville, but it did lead him to the adventure he craved. After three months at Camp S-133, spent mostly planting tree seedlings, he requested a transfer to Idaho. There he spent two years at forestry work, building fire towers and learning the electrical trade. At the tender age of 17, he left the CCC to train as a forest ranger in Missoula, Montana. He became a forest firefighter in Idaho, and during World War II saw a lot of action with the 82nd Airborne, including a D-Day leap into France. With a penchant for high places, Hank became a skyscraper window washer in New York City after the war. Like Leonard Monteleone, he returned to the Catskills to hunt and vacation, and ultimately bought some land and built a log cabin. Ironically, he said, the logs came from Idaho.[15]

In the autumn of 1937, Camp S-133 was again threatened with closure, but a community letter-writing campaign and lobbying by Forest Ranger Furch and Camp Superintendent John F. Paul helped keep it open. Camps at Hartwick and Tannersville were closed instead.[16] Men from Company 1230 were assigned the task of dismantling the latter facility.

Always, there were trees to plant. Explained Stanton Hogan: "One guy had a mattock, lifted the dirt back and took two or three big steps. The following guy had a sack in front of him with the trees. He'd put one in the hole, stomp dirt around it, and move to the next hole. The trees were maybe a foot long and came in bundles of about a hundred. At the end of the day, some guys hid the leftovers under rocks."[17]

A beautiful plantation of red pine and white spruce was planted along Millbrook Road in an area known as Kelly Hollow. The state had acquired the land from Corbett & Stuart, wood acid factory owners who had logged the former Gavette-Johnson farm. The CCC replanted it and built stone-lined ponds to provide water for combating future fires.[18] This may have been the 21-acre plantation, described in the 1937 Conservation Department Annual Report, which was thinned and pruned as a demonstration of silvicultural treatment to encourage crop trees. In the Denver Valley, Henry Newell and other enrollees established a plantation that is now enjoyed by his nephew, Bob Reed, who has a cabin across the valley.[19]

Back at camp the mess hall menu was simple: hearty food and plenty of it. "We'd have breakfast after roll call. There'd be eight men at a table," said Robert Barnes. "Oatmeal, scrambled eggs, maybe home fries, a big dish of stewed prunes in the middle of the table. And pancakes. We called 'em 'blow out patches' because you could almost use 'em to patch a tire. If you could get 'em down, they'd hold you till noon."

In the field there'd be sandwiches, and coffee kept hot over an open fire. Barnes's favorite dinner was spaghetti. "We had Italian cooks and they could really make a good meat sauce. On Fridays we'd have scallops or seafood. Can you imagine that? You never left the mess hall hungry. We all gained weight."

A menu of educational classes ranging from meat cutting to typing to salesmanship was offered three evenings a week. Guest speakers from the community came in monthly. A library of 750 mostly donated books was established. (Enrollees built the education building to house the library, but didn't complete it until August 1938, just a couple of months before the camp closed.[20])

Enrollees were allowed into Margaretville to attend church services; Jewish services were offered at camp. The May 1936 camp inspection report noted, "A bond between the camp and the local churches has been made through the joint production of Biblical plays." Indeed, training in diction, movement and acting was pro-

vided by a dramatic instructor, who also gave music lessons and
directed a "glee club."

There were ping-pong and weekly movies at camp. Michael
Strada remembers going to the local Galli-Curci Theater to see
"Goldwyn Follies." In April 1938, the company hosted an open

*The work didn't
stop just because
the snow fell.
Stanton Hogan
took this photo of
friends, then was
himself photo-
graphed cooking
lunch for the crew.*

house to celebrate the fifth anniversary of the CCC. The public was invited to a vaudeville show at the camp.[21]

Athletic diversions included boxing, baseball, track and field, and soccer. Howard Etts Jr. was a pitcher on the Margaretville High School baseball team and a forward on the soccer team,

Margaretville CCC workers carved miles of hiking and skiing trails on Pakatakan Ridge, as well as in Woodland Valley, Ulster County, where they teamed with Boiceville enrollees to develop Woodland Valley State Campsite. Stanton Hogan

which practiced against the CCC. "They had pretty good teams, big, strong boys, good hitters," he recalled. "But we could out-run them, because they wore their CCC uniforms and big clunky shoes. We played behind the A&P and sold 25¢ tickets for Saturday games."[22] A dance, a basketball game between the Margaretville and Tannersville CCC teams, and a couple of boxing exhibitions offered a cabin fever remedy in January 1936 when the local camp invited the public to Todd's Hall in Arkville.[23]

Some enrollees sought their entertainment elsewhere. "We'd walk a mile uptown to Levy's beer joint, or hitch a ride to dances up in Vega or at Locust Grove," said Robert Barnes. "Beer was a nickel a glass," added Lou Kole. "They saw the uniform, they didn't ask your age." Bill Sanford of Halcottsville said he would occasion-ally pick up a truckload of CCC workers and take them to that hamlet to dances at Kelly's Hall. He remembered that there were sometimes fisticuffs. Yes, Barnes said, and sometimes on Monday morning the camp's captain would have to go to Delhi to get the offenders out of jail.

Most, though, were too tired to get into trouble. They might hitchhike home to see their families on weekends off. Or they had other interests. Robert Barnes found his at the general store run by his uncle, Harrison Barnes, in Arkville. There he met 17-year-old Cora Oliver, who became Robert's wife. In the fall of 1938, the Margaretville camp was being phased out but "there was still no work. I didn't have a nickel. So I re-upped for another six months, went west to Moab, Utah, where we worked on livestock watering systems for public grazing lands." He returned to Cora and they were married for 50 years.

Michael Strada came back to Margaretville in 2004 to see if he could find the place where, in 1938, he had come when he left his Italian immigrant parents in the Bronx and set off to make his own way in the world. "I wanted to join the Navy, but my

Ski Fever

It's no exaggeration to say that the CCC was instrumental in introducing skiing to the Catskills.

In the 1930s, as interest in outdoor recreation boomed, the State Conservation Department created campsites, lean-tos and hiking trails throughout the region. Following the 1932 Third Winter Olympics in Lake Placid, skiing became all the rage, and the state did its best to provide winter sport opportunities, using CCC labor.

Selectively cutting trees on state lands, CCC enrollees broadened and smoothed existing hiking trails and woods roads to accommo-date skiers who carried their boards to the top of a hill or mountain and skied down. Dual-use trails built from 1935 to 1937 included Pakatakan Ridge near Margaretville, Hunter Mountain and adjacent Diamond Notch, and a nine-mile trail from the head of Woodland Valley over Panther Mountain to Allaben in the Town of Shandaken.

Thousands of city dwellers took the train to Phoenicia to try out the first mechanized downhill ski area in New York State, built largely by Margaretville CCC enrollees.
Lonnie Gale

A man identified only as L. Laratta gets his ski legs in Phoenicia. Joseph Monteleone

The *Catskill Mountain News* of January 3, 1936, described an assortment of new ski trails, adding, "At Pine Hill the objective of all skiers will be the Belle Ayre run built and maintained by the department which starts at the fire tower at the summit of the mountain and ends in Pine Hill village." Later that year the CCC was enlisted to work on the Belle Ayre trail.

By 1938 the Conservation Department counted 139 miles of ski trails on State Forest Preserve lands in the Adirondacks and Catskills. Forty thousand copies of a booklet, "Ski Trails of New York," were printed and distributed that year.

Private ski clubs had also sprung up to develop hillside winter playgrounds. The February 14, 1936, *Catskill Mountain News* reported that the Fleischmanns Chapter of the Catskill Mountain Ski Club had been organized to obtain rights of way from private property owners to establish a trail from Lake Switzerland "along the mountains to the Wallace Crosby slopes in Halcott Center." The paper also featured a map showing five ski areas near Phoenicia, including the Simpson Memorial Ski Slope.

Carroll Simpson and friends Lloyd Kinsey and Paul Miller had been spectators at the Lake Placid Olympics and came home fired up about the prospects for developing the sport on their home turf, where another enthusiast, Harold Ring, built an exciting, but financially unsuccessful, ski jump.

Artist Jack Rivolta, working for the Works Projects Administration, created this poster promoting New York State as a haven for skiers and winter sports enthusiasts. Library of Congress

THEY LIKE WINTER IN NEW YORK STATE
THE STATE THAT HAS EVERYTHING

BUREAU OF STATE PUBLICITY — CONSERVATION DEPT.— LITHGOW OSBORNE, COMMISSIONER — ALBANY, N.Y.

In December 1935, nine members of the Simpson family deeded to the state six acres of land near the entrance to Woodland Valley. This made it possible for the CCC to clear a trail with its base alongside a spur of the New York Central Railroad tracks. Margaretville CCC Company 1230 worked on the project during early 1936. Stanton Hogan recalls carrying dynamite up the slopes to blast rocks and tree stumps out of the trail, a dangerous job that left a fellow CCC member dead.

"The foreman had supposedly blown the whistle to warn the crew they were going to touch the dynamite off," Hogan related. "One guy ran into a lean-to to get out of the way. The boulder blew up in the air, came through the roof of the lean-to and killed him." Edward Reynolds, 17, of Brooklyn, died from his injuries. A co-worker, Anthony Martorano, 20, suffered a fractured skull.

In late January 1936, the railroad began sending weekend trains filled with hundreds of skiers to the Simpson Memorial Ski Slope, named in honor of Jay H. Simpson, a State Forest Ranger from 1915 to 1919. A mechanized rope tow, the first in the state, had been fashioned from the rear wheels of a Buick and a bunch of pulleys, so getting to the top of the two—and-a-half-mile trail was a bit easier.

The slope was a big attraction for several years and inspired civic boosters in Tannersville to build a 2,000-foot ski run near Rip Van Winkle Lake, where CCC Company 291 had camped from 1934 to 1937. "The investment is slight compared to the amount spent to boost Tannersville as a summer resort. Mother Nature has donated the surroundings gratis," trumpeted George Meyer in a newsletter called *Tannersville Topics*. "Phoenicia was looked upon as an experiment which proved that winter sports are popular and that not all its enthusiasts care to journey to the Adirondacks for their fun."

However, the Simpson slope was closed more than it was open during World War II when gas rationing made it hard to run the rope tows. After the war, people preferred cars over trains and took their ski business elsewhere, often to New England where the CCC had been employed blazing ski trails and access roads on Mt. Washington in New Hampshire, Mt. Mansfield in Stowe, Vermont, and on several other mountains in Maine, Massachusetts and Connecticut.

It wasn't long before the State of New York got in on the action, opening Whiteface Ski Center in the Adirondacks in 1947 and Belleayre Ski Center in the Catskills in 1950. Many privately operated ski centers were also developed and continue to enhance the Catskill Region's reputation as a prime destination within easy reach of millions of skiers.

Conservation Dept. Annual Reports 1936–42; *Ski History*, Winter 1996; *SKI Magazine*, Dec. 1994; *Woodstock Times*, Dec. 1, 1988; *Catskill Mountain News*, Jan. 3, 17, 31, Feb. 14, Nov. 20, 27 and Dec. 11, 1936; interview with Stanton Hogan, Jan. 24, 2004; Deed, James A. Simpson et al to People of State of New York, Dec. 9, 1935; "Rip Van Winkle Awoke in 1935," *Tannersville Topics* (undated, believed 1938)

It wasn't all work and no play in the CCC camps. This merry band was all dressed up for a night on the town.
Joseph Monteleone

mother wouldn't let me. So I joined the CCC. I'd hoped to go to Oregon or Idaho or Washington. But they sent me here. Still, I liked the country, the mountains. We did some hard work, and it made me rugged."

Indeed, at age 84, he could still hold his own walking through the Huckleberry Brook forest he had thinned and planted as a strapping teenager. But he did not recognize the site of Camp S-133 on Old Route 28 south of Margaretville. After it was closed on October 22, 1938, Strada and fellow enrollees were sent to Masonville. The buildings were reportedly sold to Max Silverstein. who dismantled them and used the lumber for other projects. The land was subsequently mined for gravel and top soil. It is overgrown with brush and scrub trees. No trace of the camp remains.

CHAPTER 10
FROM FARMS TO FOREST

MASONVILLE, CAMP S-100
DELAWARE COUNTY
MAY 22, 1934–
JANUARY 13, 1936;
OCTOBER 22, 1938–
NOVEMBER 18, 1941

For a couple of years before CCC Company 299 moved to Masonville, the state had been buying land in the vicinity with an eye to planting trees. Armed with a 1931 legislative mandate (see Chapter 1) and a million dollars in what was to be the first of an 11-year program of land acquisition for reforestation, Conservation Department forestry officials fanned out in 1932 to collect abandoned farms.

"In the Town of Masonville, on one road in a former school district, there are ten farms which a few years ago were owned by well-to-do, prosperous farmers," reported the *Delaware Express* on July 1, 1932. "For the past few years, the farms have been unoccupied, and recently nine of the farms were sold to the state for reforesting. One was sold by Katherine Colvin Winters. The farm has been owned by the Colvin family for nearly 100 years."

The Colvin homestead was among 174,000 acres purchased by the state in 1932 for $673,000—$3.87 an acre. But then the Depression hit the state's pocketbook, too, and annual appropriations for land buys and reforestation were slashed to $400,000 a year for the next several years. Enter the federal government and the ready labor of the CCC, just in time to cover the Colvin farm and hundreds like it with forests of green. Because of the funding shortfall, land was acquired only if it was within the working limits of a CCC camp.[1]

In Masonville that camp was S-100. Its goal? To plant two million trees on 10,000 to 12,000 acres of newly acquired State Forest lands in the Delaware County area.[2] The camp existed for nearly seven years. It was occupied from 1934–36 by Company 299, and from 1938–41 by Company 1230. The camp remained vacant for two years in between.

Company 299 arrived at the campsite on Route 8 between Sidney and Deposit in the midst of a rollicking thunderstorm on May 22, 1934. They lived in tents that first summer, but built wooden barracks and other buildings by fall. Two excellent springs supplied the camp. "There is no finer water to be found in Delaware County, as many hunters familiar with the region well know," said the *Deposit Courier* on August 23, 1934. (The newspaper later produced by Masonville CCC members was aptly named *The Cold Springer*.)

Captain Ralph Schultz, an Army Engineer Corps reservist, was commanding officer of Camp S-100. Royal G. Bird supervised forestry personnel and "Local Experienced Men" (LEMs), including five crew foremen, a tractor operator, a surveyor, a mechanic and a blacksmith.[3]

Many enrollees in the initial Masonville contingent of 115 had been with Company 299 through previous assignments at Glacier National Park in Montana during the summer of 1933, and at Manassas, Virginia, the following winter.[4] One of them was Steve Egnaczak from Olean, New York. One of eight children of immigrant parents, Steve enrolled in the CCC in 1933 when his father was injured. A younger brother also joined the CCC. Steve sent his $25-a-month CCC pay home to support his siblings. According to his sister-in-law, Marian Egnaczak, he left the corps when he found steady work in 1935 at Scintilla, a Sidney factory that made aircraft engine parts.

The CCC "veterans'" ranks in Masonville were filled out by another 100 enrollees funneled from training camps, and by local youth recruited by the county's reemployment office.

The camp consisted of 14 buildings, including five barracks, quarters for army and conservation officers, a mess hall, bath-house, infirmary, recreation hall, education building, garages, a blacksmith shop, and storehouses. The buildings were arranged around a central muster field with a tall flagpole.[5]

The men of Company 299 not only built the camp, they planted a phenomenal number of trees, mostly red pine and Norway spruce. The Dec. 29, 1934, issue of *Happy Days*, the national CCC newspaper, noted that Company 299 had planted 1,160,000 seedlings to date, "an average of 507 trees per man per day for crews totaling 88 men."

In its 20-month stay at Masonville, Company 299 reforested more than 1,600 acres, built 12 miles of truck trails, cleared 43 miles of fire line, dug 38 stone-lined water holes for firefighting, thinned 700 acres of woodland, constructed trout pools and

CCC Camp S-100 is seen in this aerial view. State Route 8 is the principal highway crossing the frame. NYS Archives

planted shade trees along a mile and a half of stream, surveyed 30 miles of boundary line for a new purchase area, and put up 650 rods of barbed wire boundary fence.[6]

CCC workers were called out to assist Delhi, Walton and Franklin residents whose homes and farms were damaged in disastrous flooding in the summer of 1935. Despite the circumstances, the contact between local residents and enrollees was described as "a most pleasant one" by the *Walton Reporter*. "The one thing that has the most favorable impression about the CCC boys during the past week is how they apparently like to work. It mattered little how dirty the work or how difficult, the boys tackled it with a grin. They acted as if they enjoyed it. Most of us had no real idea of what kind of people there were in the CCC camps before the flood, but now we know they are good clean American boys who are willing to take any kind of a job while waiting for a position."[7]

Early on, the young men were sometimes regarded with suspicion and even disdain by local residents.* Referendum voters in the Sidney school district turned down a request by the camp to use the school gym for basketball games in 1934. They later changed their minds, allowing the gym to be used and also providing space for night classes taught by CCC Education Director Daniel Harris and attended by 200 enrollees as well as local people. Camp arts and crafts instructor Eugene Badger directed a group of enrollees in making an eight-by-eight-foot map of the camp vicinity showing historical sites and points of interest.[8]

The money circulated by enrollees, LEMs and officers, and through local purchases of food and supplies, was certainly welcomed. The *Sidney Record*, announcing the opening of the camp

---

*Perhaps the residents of Sidney felt a bit overwhelmed by relief efforts in their midst: Camp Sidney, a transient camp under the auspices of the Works Progress Administration (WPA), housed 200 adult workers from the New York City area at a former silk mill on Sherman Avenue in the village. The men built a new municipal reservoir, sidewalks, and other amenities, according to articles in the *Sidney Record* during 1936.

*A Masonville CCC
crew at work.*
Sanford Shelton

on May 31, 1934, happily predicted that $5,000 a month would cross local palms.

To improve relations with the community, the camp hosted an "inaugural dance" in its new rec hall in November 1934. Captain Schultz and staff extended a special invitation to Sidney residents to come get acquainted and dance to the music of Goodrich and his Red Caps. That winter, CCC trucks equipped with snowplows helped clear winter roads for farmers and townspeople.[9]

Company 299 proved itself a good neighbor. And then it was time to leave. In January 1936, the camp was shuttered and the men moved to Narrowsburg on the Delaware River, where they would continue their tree planting ways on the 14,000-acre Ten Mile River Boy Scout Camp and environs (see Ten Mile River).

Camp S-100 sat idle until October 22, 1938, when Company 1230 moved in, leaving Margaretville Camp S-133 to be dismantled.

Douglas "Red" Charles was with the advance crew from Margaretville that went to Masonville to ready the mothballed camp for its new occupants. Born in 1921, he was one of nine children whose sick mother struggled alone to care for them in a rented house in Fish's Eddy in western Delaware County. He enrolled in the CCC in June 1938. His paycheck supported his family back

*Dominick August
digging for his
supper at the
Masonville camp.*
Dominick August

home while he enjoyed plenty of food and was outfitted with a dress uniform, work clothes, work shoes and "Arctics" (galoshes) that fitted over them, a warm mackinaw coat and work gloves.

In the fall of 1938, the company moved across the county to Masonville, and Charles was appointed night watchman to make sure the wood and coal stoves didn't go out on cold winter nights in the garages, shop buildings and forestry personnel barracks. A fair hand with an axe and a saw, he cut dead trees and planted more live ones than he cared to remember during his 18 months at Masonville.[10]

A major project Charles and his compatriots worked on was Beaverkill State Campground, first opened in 1928. To further develop the campground, CCC Company 1230 in Margaretville set up a tent camp there in 1936 (see Chapter 9). The company continued to

A flagpole stood at the center of Camp 100 in Masonville.
Sanford Shelton

occupy the side camp after its relocation to Masonville. The side camp was 42 miles from the main camp. The work went on there each year from March to October through 1941. In addition to the campground amenities, the project included construction of piers, deflectors, and rock pools to improve the nearby Beaverkill and Willowemoc streams, both legendary trout fisheries.[11]

In 1939 the Conservation Department Annual Report recorded 16,868 visitors to the expanded Beaverkill Campsite. It was a banner year for state parks and campgrounds (officially called "camp-

Like most CCC camps, Masonville had its own baseball team that competed against other CCC camps and community teams.
Dominick August

sites" at that time), with more than 742,000 people spending some time at an outdoor facility, compared to 50,000 just 12 years earlier, when attendance records began.

Herbert Call was the principal foreman of Camp S-100. Several LEMs, including Art Hill and Jim Minnerly, commuted for a time from their homes in Margaretville and Roxbury to Masonville, but it was a long way to the new camp, and some decided it wasn't worth it.

That didn't stop the work, though. A report on jobs completed by Camp S-100 between October 24, 1938, and July 31, 1939, included one dwelling (a ranger cabin at the Beaverkill), erection of 123 signs and markers, 25 tables and benches, beach improvement, a mile of stream development, and installation of 663 rods of fencing. And always, there were trees: 1,165 acres planted, 231 acres of forest stand improvement, 5 miles of road and trailside fire hazard reduction, and more than 1,200 acres scouted for tree pests and diseases.[12]

Captain Robert Fava was assigned command of the company in September 1938. When he left the service a year later, Lieutenant George Schuyler took over. His tenure was cut short after an inspector, on a surprise visit, discovered him sound asleep after a drinking binge while four enrollees had a beer party in the officers' quarters.[13]

Another unfortunate incident involved the death of "Smiley" Burnette, a local enrollee. Assigned to a road building crew, he was working alongside a dump truck that began to roll. Believing there was no one behind the wheel, he attempted to climb into the cab to stop the truck and was pulled under the wheels.[14]

For the most part, though, there were few injuries. Dr. Elliot Danforth of Sidney was the contract physician for the camp. "He would never fail to go out of his way to pick up CCC boys going and coming from camp," related one enrollee. "He would stop at the post office and at the railroad station to see if anyone needed a ride back to camp. I can still hear his soft voice saying, 'Get in, gang.'"[15]

Masonville was a model CCC camp. About a third of the enrollees regularly attended vocational training and classes in such things as typing, photography, woodworking, auto mechanics, arithmetic, even etiquette. A 1,200-book library was heavily used. The recreation hall contained ping-pong and pool tables, a radio and a piano. There were weekly movies, musical performances and the occasional square dance ("It would have been perfect if

The Beaverkill State Campsite near Livingston Manor in Sullivan County, first estab-
lished in 1928 and shown above in the 1930 Conservation Department Annual Report,
was expanded and developed with CCC labor from 1936 through 1941. Company 1230
established a temporary tent camp there while assigned to Margaretville, and continued
working at it (below) once the company moved to Masonville. Joseph Monteleone

Who *Were* These Guys?

Russ Gundelach was a CCC enrollee who served in Masonville during 1940. In correspondence with Sanford Shelton, a retired Pennsylvania park superintendent and a CCC historian, Gundelach provided vivid descriptions of people and events he remembered from his time at Camp S-100. The following are excerpts from his letters, written from Westfield, New York, in 1992 and 1993:

"The Captain did all he could to improve our lot. He once got someone to donate a good piano and he sent a truck and eight men into Binghamton to pick it up. He needed the piano for a big dance party to be held in the rec room. He coerced the owners of the bakery in Binghamton that supplied the camp with bread (over 2,500 loaves per month) to send about 40 girls and chaperones to our party. We had a good time. One can see why the Captain was so well liked.

"Norm Applegate was my immediate boss for most of the time I was in camp as I was a truck driver. Norm looked close to 40 and came from an upstate city. He told us that before getting into the Cs he could not find a job so he slept all day and spent his nights drinking coffee in all-night restaurants with his tools in his car. He kept a regular schedule in moving from one restaurant to another so police and gas stations could find him to make emergency repairs. Even paid for his coffee and meals by working on the cars of the restaurant people.

"Nick Raesner looked to be in his middle 50s. Good woodsman. He had been a butcher at one time and taught meat cutting. It was kind of a game trying to swipe meat from his class to cook at noon in the field. He was also a hunter and fisherman and taught kids how to make belts from rattlesnake skins (took two to make a belt.)

"One of the chainmen on the surveying crew, a great big kid named Bill, awoke about 5 one morning with intolerable belly cramps. He was promptly loaded into our ambulance and was sent

An unidentified CCC enrollee looked the part of the troubadour. Many young men brought their instruments when they joined the corps, and most camps had a resident band or orchestra. Sanford Shelton

to the hospital at Bainbridge for an appendectomy. There he was given a dose of oil and the next day, after being thoroughly cleaned out, was sent back to camp. Bill later told us that the night before he had got up to go to the latrine. When outside he could smell goodies baking. He sneaked down to the mess hall and could see old Mac placing trays of doughnuts on the hall tables to cool. Bill managed to swipe a whole tray full and ate them all. When the cramps started he did not dare tell about the doughnuts, but at Bainbridge he was afraid they might really cut him open so he confessed all.

"Sal was a black guy from Brooklyn. Most everyone liked Sal immensely, of course there were a few who resented a black guy being so much smarter than the rest of us, and he was. He had had voice training and sang beautifully, a baritone. He sang with the choir in the church at Masonville. He was raised 'white' and would have nothing to do with other blacks. The group Sal enlisted with told me that when told he was going to a black camp, he put up such a fuss they let him go with the white guys. [See "Racial Segregation."]

"There was O'Reilly, 18 years of age, red hair, freckles, a brogue and cross-eyes. From Brooklyn, he grew up in an orphanage and at age 16 was on his own with no job and no skills. So he joined the Cs and was there two years, the maximum time allowed. His pay had been held in escrow and when discharged he was given a train ticket, seven dollars in cash, and a check in the amount of $600, a veritable fortune at the time. He loved the CCC, and no wonder.

"Joe was allowed to enter, and stay, in the CCC despite the fact that one leg was a full four inches shorter than the other. He walked with the most peculiar gait I've ever seen. At the Father Baker Orphanage in Buffalo he was fitted with a built up shoe which he refused to wear on the streets because, in his words, 'It scared little kids.' He and his pal Eddie applied to the CCC. Joe was turned down, while Eddie was accepted. Joe put on the best act of his life, with real tears running down his cheeks as he pleaded on his knees for admittance. No one had the heart to hold him back. On their arrival in camp they looked like a couple of scarecrows. Neither weighed more than a hundred pounds. Joe asked for a chance to prove he could do as much as anyone despite his handicap. He worked like a horse. Six months later these kids were new people, weighing about 160 pounds and all muscle. The two spent the summer in the shale pit, Joe on the jack hammer, Eddie swinging a sledge hammer. In the winter, they worked together as a cross-cut saw team. They could fell trees as fast as the two-year men."

Letters excerpted with permission from Sanford Shelton

Beaverkill State Campground (as it is now known) is noted for its covered bridge, its awesome fishing, and its signature stone walls, shown here under construction by a CCC crew. Joseph Monteleone

some of the fellows had been of the opposite sex," was the wry report in a March 1941 issue of *The Cold Springer*).

There were regular trips to town for roller skating at two Sidney rinks. Some men were on local bowling leagues, others competed in inter-barracks basketball, volleyball and baseball contests.

Boxing was a popular diversion. Dominick August, one of five CCC sons of Italian immigrants, had learned the science of dodging and weaving at a Schenectady boys camp as an 11-year-old. As a teenager he boxed for money (50¢ or a dollar), later taking on all comers at the CCC. In February 1941, "Punchy" August

Ten Mile River

If they hadn't gotten their fill of planting trees and digging fire lines at Masonville, Company 299 was in for more of the same at Narrowsburg.

Camp S(P)-85 was located at Ten Mile River Boy Scout Camps, a collection of campgrounds owned by the Boy Scout Foundation of New York along the Delaware River in Sullivan County. Hundreds of acres there had been burned over and needed to be cleared of dead trees and replanted. A 30-foot firebreak was cleared around the 50-mile perimeter of the scout property, and existing trails and logging roads were improved to permit firefighting access into the interior of the 12,000-acre camp that was spread over four towns.

While the property was (and remains) privately owned by the Boy Scout Foundation, it was considered eligible for CCC assistance because of the regional need for forest remediation and fire protection. However, it may have been the only CCC camp in the country actually

The CCC camp at Ten Mile River Boy Scout Camps near Narrowsburg had an impressive entrance. Ed Gettel and Ten Mile River Scout Museum

sited on private land. The fact that FDR was an avid Boy Scout sup-
porter may have prompted this exception; he had helped establish the
Boy Scout Foundation (later called the Greater New York Councils of
Boy Scouts).

In August, 1933, FDR paid a visit to Ten Mile River and addressed
2,500 boys and their leaders:

> This Spring, because of my Scout training, I took a leaf out of
> the notebook of Scouting in order to take care of a lot of boys
> who are a bit older than you are—boys who had graduated
> from high school and some of them from college but who had
> not been able to get work for a year or two or three years. We
> started in this country, modeling it a lot after Scouting, a Civilian
> Conservation Corps, and today there are two or three hundred
> thousand older boys taking care of forests, preventing forest
> fires, stopping soil erosion and doing a thousand other tasks that
> the country needs.

Three months after his speech, in November 1933, Camp S-85
was established at Ten Mile River. It was occupied for a year by a
company of junior men. A company of veterans from Barre, Vermont, was stationed there from October 1934 through January
1936. In addition to fire prevention work, CCC members of Camp
S-85 scoured the region for white pine blister rust carriers and laid
out some new campsites to accommodate the 15,000 to 20,000
urban Boy Scouts whose troops had access to the facilities. "Such
a vacationland affords a great opportunity for the presentation to
these youths of the true and essential value of forests and wild life,"
explained the *Delaware Valley News* April 3, 1936.

In early 1936 a contingent of 175 young men from Company 299
of Masonville replaced the veterans at Camp S-85. But they barely got
settled before the order came to close the Narrowsburg camp. When it

shut down in April 1936, peripatetic Company 299 was off again, this time to Texas to do battle with soil erosion and dust storms.

The Ten Mile River Scout Museum at the camp in Narrowsburg contains exhibits and information on the CCC's work there from 1933 to 1936. You can also visit a virtual museum at www.tmrmuseum.org.

Delaware Valley News; Camp S-85 inspection reports; *Scouting Magazine,* October 1933; Executive Order 6160, June 7, 1933

A CCC wood-cutting crew takes a break at Ten Mile River Boy Scout Camps. A 30-foot fire break was cleared around the 50-mile perimeter of the Sullivan County facility to reduce the likelihood of destructive blazes. Ed Gettel and Ten Mile River Scout Museum

scored four knockouts to take the welterweight title in a Binghamton match attended by 2,000 people and organized by State Police Troop C stationed in Sidney.[16]

In a memoir written later in life, August recalled the bean sandwiches, the trees left under rocks, the "whistle crazy" top kick (sergeant), the illicit football games played when they were supposed to be at church. Among other things, "The CCC taught me to be obedient, pay attention, make a bunk and make it right!"

How to do laundry, too. Red Charles said, "That was one of the things we dreaded. We washed our own clothes with scrub boards and hung them outdoors or over the rafters in the barracks. Luckily they did the bedding for us."

The work continued that spring and summer, but there was

change in the wind. Enrollees signed up for "National Defense" night courses at the local high school to learn mechanical or industrial trades to prepare them for war manufacturing jobs, jobs that were

Doug "Red" Charles posed with his handiwork on a visit to Beaverkill State Campground. As a young man, he helped build the stone walls and campsites. He is in the second row, fifth from left, in this 1939 group portrait of the side camp crew.
Doug Charles

luring young men away from the woods and into the factories. Many "graduated" and took advantage of those jobs in Sidney, Binghamton, Schenectady and elsewhere. Still more doffed the CCC uniform and donned Army greens.

Investigator Patrick King's inspection of Camp S-100 in October of 1941 pegged company strength at just 77 men. His concluding comments tried to put the best face on it: "Although this camp has been greatly reduced in company strength, there seems to be a spirit that carries on and a determination to do their best, come what may."

But in November 1941, the order to close came to both the Masonville camp and the Breakabeen camp up in Schoharie County. More than eight productive years after it was launched, the Civilian Conservation Corps in the Catskills had come to an end.

3,693,492 Trees

"According to a report received by J. A. Lennox, county club agent from the Conservation Department, there were planted in Delaware County during the past year 3,693,492 trees. They were planted as follows: 90,000 by 4-H Club members; 13,000 by agricultural high school members; 2,000 by the Franklin Central Rural School; 100 by Shankitunk 4-H Camp; 1,000 by Walton public schools; 11 by the Delaware County Fair; 3,539,734 by the CCC camp members on state property; and 48,000 by private land owners. This is the largest amount ever set in any one year in Delaware County and is an excellent start towards the planting of the 200,000,000 trees estimated by state foresters that need to be planted in the county."

Delaware Express, Delhi, January 25, 1935

CHAPTER 11
THE END OF THE CCC

Following the closure of the Breakabeen and Masonville camps in the fall of 1941, the CCC continued for another few months elsewhere in New York and across the United States, but the end was nigh.

In early 1941 there were 300,000 CCC enrollees across the country. Ten months later there were just 160,000 men in 900 camps. Six thousand men each month were leaving for employment outside the CCC, many at defense plants.[1]

Across New York State, CCC enrollments dwindled as well, even though eligibility rules had eased again and the amount of the monthly pay they were allowed to keep had gone from $5 a month to $8. It just wasn't enough to entice great numbers of new enrollees, and so the camps closed one after another. At the end of 1941, only 23 camps were assigned to the State Conservation Department Lands and Forests Division. In January 1942, there were just ten.[2]

The demise of the CCC, FDR's pet program, was debated in Congress and in the press in early 1942. In the weeks following the United States' entry into World War II, the president and others argued that while the economic emergency had passed, the CCC would prove useful in plane spotting, firefighting in case of bombings or sabotage, and in preparing young men for the rigors of the military. Detractors said the program's usefulness had ended and continuing to spend money on it would be wasteful and duplicative.

In a March 25 letter to CCC Director James McIntee, who had taken over after the death of Robert Fechner in 1940, Roosevelt used the occasion of the ninth anniversary of the CCC's establishment to congratulate him for his fine work. "There is a real place for the CCC during this emergency and it will be called upon more and more to perform tasks which will strengthen our country, and aid in the successful operation of the war. Many of the young men now in the camps will enter the nation's armed forces. When that time comes, they will be better prepared to serve their country because of the discipline, the training and the physical hardihood they have gained in the Civilian Conservation Corps."[3]

This photo of a truckload of weary CCC workers speaks volumes about the hard physical labor performed by millions of young men on conservation and construction projects nationwide. Joseph Monteleone

But the corps would not see its tenth anniversary.

After months of wrangling with Congress, the President asked for an appropriation of $149,000,000 to maintain 150 CCC camps for the fiscal year 1942–43. On June 2 the House of Representatives voted 158–151 not to appropriate further money, and instead to provide $500,000 to liquidate the agency. On June 26, after much dramatic debate, the Senate voted 32 against and 32 in favor of the appropriation. Thirty-two senators did not vote. Vice President Henry Wallace used his tie-breaking vote to uphold the CCC. But in subsequent House-Senate Conference Committee meetings to resolve the impasse, Senate representatives receded from their June 26 action, effectively killing the CCC.[4]

Members of CCC Company 1230 based at Margaretville Camp 133 pose at a job site in Huckleberry Brook. Stanton Hogan

Many CCC camps, like the one at Laurens, sent enrollees out to survey state land boundaries.
NYS CCC Museum

In New York State the Conservation Department's own ranks had been drastically reduced with the advent of World War II. The Annual Report for 1942 showed that 209 employees were in the service, and 37 others had been given leaves to work in war industries. Rangers and wardens who remained on the job spent a lot of time spotting for enemy airplanes from fire towers and performing other unnamed defense activities. Many of the state parks and campsites on which the CCC had worked so hard did not open in 1942 for lack of manpower to staff and maintain them, not that there were many folks with the leisure to go camping.

At the start of the spring planting season, only two CCC camps were available for reforestation efforts. They gamely soldiered on, planting 2,089,500 trees in Oneida and Chenango Counties. In July 1942, CCC camps at North Pharsalia and at the Plattsburgh air base closed their doors. So did the camp at Paul Smiths, which survived the longest in the state—from June 1933 through July 22, 1942. The last CCC operation in New York, at Speculator in the Adirondacks, finally shut down in October 1942.

The Conservation Department did get some help from a new type of camp—a Civilian Public Service camp in Cooperstown—

where conscientious objectors to the military draft were assigned to reforestation and other tasks previously done by the CCC.[5] But there would never again be a period of such phenomenal accomplishment on the public lands of the state.

> "The conservation program of New York State has been advanced many years by the substantial contribution made by the CCC," said the department's 1942 Report to the Legislature. "Since 1933, approximately $9,000,000 have been spent on CCC work under the direction of the Divisions of Lands and Forests and Fish and Game. Slightly over half of this total amount has been spent for the supervision of enrollees. The remainder has been spent for purchase of supplies and materials, operation of equipment, etc. ... [This] could not have been done for many years to come with regular appropriations."[6]

So what exactly did the leaders and men of the CCC do for New York?

The Legacy[*]

Camps designated for work in state and private forests, state parks and military reservations, and those earmarked for Soil Conservation Service and Army Corps of Engineers projects employed 220,752 men (209,775 junior and veteran enrollees, 240 Native Americans, and 10,737 camp officers and supervisory workers).

Total estimated expenditures in New York from 1933 to 1942 were $134,563,000. Allotments to dependents by enrollees were estimated at $41,211,000.

*Statistics taken from 1941 Conservation Department Annual Report to the Legislature, and *Roosevelt's Tree Army*, by Perry Merrill

Trees planted	221,589,000
Forest stand improvement (acres)	60,152
Tree disease control (acres)	1,124,575
Tree pest control (acres)	3,781,347
Campsites and picnic grounds (acres)	1,448

Catskills: North Lake, Woodland Valley, Devil's Tombstone, Beaverkill

Truck trails (miles)	391
Vehicle bridges	73
Fire towers	19
Firefighting (man-days)	78,134
Water holes	1,207
Firebreaks (miles)	1,516
Fire hazard reduction (acres)	41,465
Bathhouses	30
Latrines/toilets	211
Camp stoves/fireplaces	2,773
Shelters (lean-tos)	51
Dams	63
Fences (rods)	144,053
Stone walls (rods)	2,552
Water supply systems	80
Pipe and tile lines (linear feet)	131,991
Signs/markers	3,928
Table/bench combinations	2,552
Foot trails	633
Horse trails	70
Stream/lake bank protection (sq. yards)	11,018
Fish-rearing ponds	107
Stream development (miles)	234
Riprap/paving (sq. yards)	3,115
Emergency work (man-days)	22,384

In addition, nearly 50 CCC camps worked on State Parks run by the Division of Parks of the NYS Conservation Department. Work tallies for those camps are not provided here.

Afterword
Youth in Conservation
since the CCC

More than two decades after the closing of Camp S-100, the New York State Division for Youth established a juvenile detention facility on the grounds of the former Masonville CCC camp. Known as Camp Brace, the residential center housed up to 60 boys, aged 16 and 17.

Doug Blakelock was conservation officer at Camp Brace. Years earlier he had picked blueberries on that very hillside, owned by the state. The CCC buildings were gone, but he could gaze across the valley to admire a mature red pine plantation established by the members of CCC Company 299 so many years before.

Now, in the mid-1960s, Blakelock took a new generation of teenaged boys into the forest. They, too, planted red pine and spruce, thinned tree stands using crosscut saws and axes, and built small deflection dams to create pools for trout. "Basically, the Camp Brace boys took care of the forests planted by the CCC," Blakelock explained in a 2004 interview. Though they were paid 50¢ a day, this was not a reemployment program like the CCC; it was a rehabilitation exercise for tough, troubled youth. Still, the effect of this outdoor manual labor on the boys of 1966 was much the same as it was for their predecessors. "It gave them a new outlook," Doug Blakelock remembered.*

*Budget cuts in the early 1970s trimmed the staff and programs at Camp Brace. Blakelock took a job at the DEC, and the conservation work ended at Camp Brace. Now known as Brace Residential Center, the facility, run by the state Office of Children and Family Services, offers vocational training in landscaping, horticulture, maintenance and other fields,

The CCC model informed and inspired a number of youth conservation programs in the decades following World War II. The Student Conservation Association (SCA) was the first such large-scale program. The brainchild of Vassar College student Elizabeth Cushman, who proposed it in her senior thesis in 1955, the SCA was launched in 1957 when the first 53 volunteers were placed in Grand Teton and Olympic National Parks. Since then SCA has engaged more than 50,000 high school, college and graduate students in all 50 states, building trails, restoring habitat, eradicating invasive species and providing other environmental services. Half a century after its founding, the New Hampshire-based organization serves 3,000 volunteers a year (www.thesca.org).

The SCA model was the basis for the Youth Conservation Corps, a federally funded program established in the late 1960s. During its height in the 1970s, it employed 32,000 young people each summer on conservation projects operated by the Departments of Interior and Agriculture as well as by states. The program was later expanded to offer year-round conservation-related jobs, but was virtually eliminated because of federal funding cuts in 1981. (www.corpsnetwork.org)

Several states, led by California in 1976, set up their own youth conservation corps. The Vermont Youth Conservation Corps is among the best known. Established in 1985, the nonprofit organization partners with federal, state, and regional agencies and organizations to employ young people in Vermont's parks and recreation areas. (www.vycc.org)

The National and Community Service Act of 1990, signed by President George H. W. Bush, created Youth Corps to give out-

and requires residents to participate in community service projects including park cleanups and nature trail maintenance in nearby communities. The center, which now accommodates 25 boys aged 12–17, is targeted for closure in January of 2009.

of-school youths full-time community service jobs. That act was amended by Congress in 1993 to create AmeriCorps. The first class of 20,000 AmeriCorps members began serving in more than 1,000 communities in September 1994. In swearing in these volunteers, President Bill Clinton said, "Service is a spark to rekindle the spirit of democracy in an age of uncertainty. When it is all said and done, it comes down to three simple questions: What is right? What is wrong? And what are we going to do about it? Today you are doing what is right—turning your words into deeds." More than 330,000 individuals have since served in AmeriCorps. (www. americorps.gov)

A local AmeriCorps unit, the Catskill Outdoor Education Corps (COEC) was established at State University of New York at Delhi in 1997. Before funding uncertainties caused its disbandment in 2007, 146 young men and women, earning modest salaries and educational stipends, created a nature trail on college property, gave outdoor recreation lessons to school groups and organizations, helped communities establish parks and public spaces, and coordinated other volunteers in tree planting, stream restoration and environmental improvement projects.

An attempt to reauthorize the Corporation for National and Community Service (CNCS) and expand its core programs, including AmeriCorps, failed in Congress on March 12, 2008, when the House of Representatives rejected by one vote a bill to expand participation to 100,000 over five years, create a summer service program for middle- and high-school students, and establish a reserve corps of AmeriCorps alumni to help out in national emergencies. And while, in his State of the Union Address in 2002, President George W. Bush asked Americans to devote two years or 4,000 hours to volunteer service during their lifetimes, and created what he called the Freedom Corps to encourage such service, his 2009 budget request for CNCS represented the fifth annual decrease for the agency.

Student Conservation Association volunteers, in the tradition of the CCC, worked on the High Falls trail at Frost Valley YMCA in Claryville, Ulster County, in June 2008. Frost Valley YMCA

Funding vagaries and political wind shifts notwithstanding, conservation volunteerism remains alive and well in the United States. There are urban corps creating gardens and parks in city centers, nonprofit groups planting willows to prevent erosion on stream banks, and homeowner associations conducting watershed cleanups. Volunteer cadres have responded in huge numbers to environmental and social emergencies like the Hurricane Katrina devastation in the Gulf Coast and severe flooding at Mt. Rainier National Park.

Massachusetts legislators adopted a bill in 2007 setting up a state-financed volunteer program that will tackle environmental problems and social issues. And the State of California, at the vanguard on this issue once again, has created the nation's first cabinet-level position for service and volunteering.

Yet there are calls to increase still further the commitment to national and community service. *Time Magazine* (September 16, 2007), the *Chicago Tribune* (March 21, 2008), *American Interest* (January–February 2008) and other publications have proposed a "National Service American Dream Account." An incentive program modeled after the GI Bill of Rights, which provided educational benefits for returning WWII veterans, the proposal would have the federal government deposit $5,000 in the name of every newborn child in the U.S. into a tax-free college education fund. Families could add to the fund, but even if they did not, interest would increase the fund to perhaps $18,000 by the time the child was of college age. The money could not be accessed, however, until the individual committed to one year of civilian or military service. If they chose not to do that, the money would return to the U.S. Treasury.

Former CCC enrollees have long clamored for a return of the program (or for some variation of it) that so shaped their lives. The National Association of CCC Alumni (now called National

Advocates for CCC Alumni), and ServeNext.org, a web-based service advocacy coalition, are among those lobbying for the environmental, social and personal benefits that service can bring.

Moreover, there are big challenges at hand, more crucial to the survival of humankind than those faced during the Depression. "Matching idealistic youth with environmental conservation work in an outdoor setting is a powerful combination," stated former New York DEC Region V Director Stu Buchanan. "This is the sort of training ground that will inspire the radical new approaches needed to solve our critical environmental challenges in the face of rapid population growth and global climate change."

The Corps Network, a nonprofit organization that links 113 service and conservation corps enrolling more than 23,000 young people each year in 41 states, is among those harkening back to the New Deal days when human potential was harnessed to snatch progress from the jaws of disaster. Says a Network spokesperson, "Like the legendary CCC of the '30s, today's Corps are a proven strategy for giving young men and women the chance to change their communities, their own lives and those of their families."

Doug Blakelock; Dave DeForest; *Chronicle of Philanthropy*, March 13, 2008; www.corpsnetwork.org

APPENDICES

APPENDIX A:

THE ALPHABET AGENCIES OF THE NEW DEAL

In 1933 President Franklin D. Roosevelt launched his "New Deal" to promote recovery and reform during the Great Depression. Among the agencies created to address various aspects of the emergency:

AAA	Agricultural Adjustment Administration, 1933
CAA	Civilian Aeronautics Authority (now Federal Aviation Administration), 1933
CCC	Civilian Conservation Corps, 1933
CCC	Commodity Credit Corporation, 1933
CWA	Civil Works Administration, 1933
FAP	Federal Art Project, part of WPA, 1935
FCA	Farm Credit Administration, 1933
FCC	Federal Communications Commission, 1934
FDIC	Federal Deposit Insurance Corporation, 1933
FERA	Federal Emergency Relief Administration, 1933
FHA	Federal Housing Administration, 1934
FMP	Federal Music Project, part of WPA 1935
FSA	Farm Security Administration, 1935
FTP	Federal Theatre Project, part of WPA 1935
FWP	Federal Writers' Project, part of WPA 1935
HOLC	Home Owners Loan Corporation, 1933
NIRA	National Industrial Recovery Act, 1933*
NLRB	National Labor Relations Board, 1934

*Title I of this act created the National Recovery Administration (NRA), which was charged with developing price and wage codes, and working hours and conditions to which all businesses in every industry would agree to adhere. It was declared unconstitutional by the U.S. Supreme Court in May 1935. Several other programs and plans were also shot down by the justices, who found FDR's centralization of government a challenge to the constitutional protection of individual and property rights.

NYA	National Youth Administration, part of WPA 1935
PRRA	Puerto Rico Reconstruction Administration, 1933
PWA	Public Works Administration, 1933
RA	Resettlement Administration, 1935
REA	Rural Electrification Administration, 1935
RFC	Reconstruction Finance Corporation (originally a Hoover agency), 1932
SEC	Securities and Exchange Commission, 1934
SSB	Social Security Board (now Social Security Administration), 1935
TVA	Tennessee Valley Authority, 1933
USHA	United States Housing Authority, 1937
WPA	Works Progress Administration, 1935

Appendix B:

CCC Camps in New York State

Between June 1933 and July 1942, a total of 161 CCC camps were established across New York State. Some operated for just a few months, others for several years. Camps were administered and maintained by the War Department (Army). There were nine corps areas in the United States; New York was in the Second Corps.

Work projects conducted by CCC companies stationed at the camps were run by various federal and state agencies, as indicated below, with oversight from the U.S. Department of Agriculture (Forestry Service and Soil Erosion/Conservation Service), and the U.S. Department of the Interior (National Park Service).

Various other work relief agencies—the Works Progress Administration (WPA), the state's Temporary Emergency Relief Administration (TERA) and the National Youth Administration—also worked on the same or parallel projects with the CCC.

Forest Camps

Projects assigned to these camps were planned and supervised by the Lands and Forests Division of the NYS Conservation Department. The camps were designated as "S" for State Forest, or "P" for Private Forest, although camps sometimes worked in both. (The CCC could work on private lands so long as the projects were for public benefit, such as forest fire protection, erosion control or pest eradication.) Lands and Forests acquired land on which it developed trails, lean-tos, fishing access sites and reforestation tracts, and created fire breaks and access roads. It also built and maintained state campgrounds (referred to as campsites during this period) in the Adirondack and Catskill Forest Preserves. The Biological Survey, a program of the Conservation Department, also supervised stream improvement projects undertaken by several of these CCC camps in proximity to state-owned streams.

S-51	Davenport (Delaware County)
S-52	Boston Corners (Columbia County)
S-53	Boiceville (Ulster County)
S-56	Fish Creek Pond (Suffolk County)
S-57	Alma Farm (Bolton Landing, Warren County)
S-58	Eighth Lake (Hamilton County)
S-59, 90	Speculator (Hamilton County)
S-60	Paul Smiths (Franklin County)
S-61	Goldsmiths (Franklin County)
S-62	Tahawus (Essex County)
S-63	Tupper Lake (Franklin County)
S-64	Schroon River (Essex County)
S-65	Burgess Farm (Bolton Landing, Warren County)
P-67	Camp Upton (Suffolk County)
S-68	Oxford (Chenango County)
P-69	Newcomb (Essex County)
P-70	Wanakena (Franklin County)
S-71, 138	Lake Placid (Essex County)
S-72	Delmar (Albany County)
S-73	Sherburne (Chenango County)
P-74	Port Henry (Essex County)
P-75	Bridgehampton (Suffolk County)
P-76	Deposit (McClure, Broome County)
S-77, 78	Cherry Plains (Rensselaer County)
S-79	Port Byron (Cayuga County)
S-80, 132	North Pharsalia (Chenango County)
S-81	Van Etten (Chemung County)
S-82	Bolton Landing (Warren County)
P-83	Boston Corners (Columbia County)

S-84	Benson Mines (Hamilton County)
S-85	Narrowsburg (Sullivan County)
S-86–89	Yaphank (Suffolk County)
S-91	N. Brookfield (Madison County)
S-92	Almond (Allegany County)
S-93	Breakabeen (Schoharie County)
S-94	Harrisville (Lewis County)
S-95	Brasher Falls (St. Lawrence County)
S-96	Homer (Cortland County)
S-97	Tannersville (Greene County)
S-98	Canajoharie (Montgomery County)
P-99	Huntington (Suffolk County)
S-100	Masonville (Delaware County)
S-101	Warrensburg (Warren County)
S-102	Plattsburg (Clinton County)
S-103	DeRuyter (Madison County)
S-104	W. Haverstraw (Rockland County)
P-105	Highland Mills (Orange County)
S-106	Salamanca (Cattaraugus County)
S-107	Minerva (Essex County)
S-108	Thendara (Herkimer County)
P-109	Elmsford (Westchester County)
S-110	Panama (Chautauqua County)
P-111	Averill Park (Rensselaer County)
P-112	Carmel (Putnam County)
S-113	Camden (Oneida County)
P-114	Johnsonville (Rensselaer County)
S-115	Indian Lake (Hamilton County)
S-116	Mannsville (Jefferson County)
S-117	Birdsall (Allegany County)
S-118	Truxton (Cortland County)
S-119	Livingstonville (Schoharie County)

S-120	Brushton (Franklin County)
P-121	Fort Ann (Washington County)
S-122	Boonville (Oneida County)
S-123	Beaverdam (Broome/Tioga Counties)
S-124	Adams (Jefferson County)
S-125	Slaterville Springs (Tompkins County)
S-126	Centerville (Allegany County)
S-127	Hartwick (Otsego County)
S-129	Newcomb (Essex County)
S-130	Williamstown (Oswego County)
S-131, S-133	Margaretville (Delaware County)
S-134	Canton (St. Lawrence County)
P-135, 136	Peekskill (Westchester County)
P-137	Sag Harbor (Suffolk County)

State Parks Camps

During the 1930s the Division of Parks of the NYS Conservation Department was responsible for seventy State Parks/state-owned campgrounds, recreation facilities and historic sites outside the Adirondack and Catskill Forest Preserves. Projects carried out at these parks were planned and supervised by staff members of twelve park commissions organized by region (Allegany, Finger Lakes, Long Island, etc.) CCC camps doing this work were sometimes set up in the parks for the duration of the projects; in other instances the camps were located nearby.

SP 1	Palisades Interstate Park—Iona Island (Rockland County)
SP 2	Harriman State Park (Rockland County)
SP 3	Lake Taghanic State Park—Ancram Columbia County)

SP 4   Taconic-Fahnestock Parks—Cold Springs
         (Putnam County)

SP 5   Letchworth State Park—Castile (Wyoming County)

SP 6   Enfield Glen State Park—Newfield
         (Tompkins County)

SP 8   Blue Mountain State Park—Cross River
         (Westchester County)

SP 9   Poundridge Reservation—Cross River
         (Westchester County)

SP 10   Selkirk Shores State Park—Pulaski (Oswego County)

SP 11   Gilbert Lake State Park—Laurens (Otsego County)

SP 12   Green Lakes State Park—Fayetteville
         (Onondaga County)

SP 13   Chenango Valley State Park—Chenango Falls
         (Broome County)

SP 16   Buttermilk Falls State Park—Ithaca
         (Tompkins County)

SP 17   Letchworth State Park—Leicester
         (Livingston County)

SP 18   Allegany State Park—Quaker Bridge
         (Cattaraugus County)

SP 19   Allegany State Park—Red House
         (Cattaraugus County)

SP 20   Palisades Interstate Park

SP 21   Bear Mountain State Park (Rockland County)

SP 22   Bear Mountain State Park (Rockland County)

SP 23   Bear Mountain State Park (Rockland County)

SP 24   Palisades Interstate Park (West Point Reservation)—
         Cornwall on the Hudson (Orange County)

SP 26   Beaver Pond—Stony Point (Rockland County)

SP 27   Palisades Interstate Park

SP 28   Palisades Interstate Park—Iona Island
         (Rockland County)

SP 29   Palisades Interstate Park

SP 30   Clarence Fahnestock Memorial Park
         (Putnam County)

SP 32   Margaret Lewis Norrie State Park—Staatsburg
         (Dutchess County)

SP 33   Fillmore Glen State Park—Moravia (Cayuga County)

SP 36   Fair Haven Beach State Park—Fair Haven
         (Cayuga County)

SP 37   Letchworth State Park—Castile (Wyoming County)

SP 38   Green Lake State Park— Fayetteville
         (Onondaga County)

SP 39   Allegany State Park—Quaker Bridge
         (Cattaraugus County)

SP 42   Croton Watershed—Goldens Bridge
         Westchester County)

SP 44   Watkins Glen State Park—Watkins Glen
         (Schuyler County)

SP 45   Cayuga State Park—Seneca Falls (Seneca County)

SP 46   Newtown Battlefield Reservation—Elmira
         (Chemung County)

SP 47   Clarence Fahnestock Memorial Park—
         (Putnam County)

SP 48   Ithaca Camp—Ithaca (Tompkins County)

SP 49   Letchworth State Park—Castile (Wyoming County)

SP 50   Allegany State Park—Red House
         (Cattaraugus County)

SP 51   Allegany State Park—Red House
         (Cattaraugus County)

SP 52   Mohansic State Park—Yorktown Heights
         (Westchester County)

SP 53   Hamlin Beach State Park—Hamlin
         (Monroe County)
SP 54   Grass Point State Park—Fishers Landing
         (Jefferson County)
SP 56   Buckhorn Island State Park—Niagara Falls
         (Niagara County)

Soil Conservation Service Camps

The earliest of these camps were supervised by the Soil Erosion Service of the U.S. Department of Agriculture. The agency's name was changed to Soil Conservation Service following passage of the Soil Conservation Act of April 1935. Companies at these camps helped farmers implement measures to reduce loss and increase nutrient value of topsoil.

SCS-1   Attica (Wyoming County)
SCS-2   Cohocton (Steuben County)
SCS-3   Kanona (Steuben County)
SCS-4   Sheds (Madison County)
SCS-5   Gallupville (Schoharie County)
SCS-6   Machias (Cattaraugus County)
SCS-7   Tioga (Tioga County)
SCS-8   Lisle (Broome County)
SCS-9   Burdett (Schuyler County)
SCS-10   Deansboro (Oneida County)
SCS-11   Big Flats (Chemung County)
SCS-12   Warsaw (Wyoming County)

Corps of Engineers, U.S. Army

Fourteen CCC camps (CE-4 through 7, and CE-9 through 18) worked on a massive flood control project in Orange County on the Wallkill River near Middletown. A Second Corps Area newsletter from June 7, 1935, indicated that eighteen companies were to be involved with this project.

Army and Military Park Camps

1, 4	Plattsburgh (Clinton County)
2	Fort Wadsworth (Richmond County)
3	Hempstead (Nassau County)
6	Carthage (Jefferson County)
7	Fort Niagara (Niagara County)
MP-1	Port Byron (Cayuga County)
MP-2	Mechanicville (Saratoga County)

NYS Conservation Department Annual Reports; Schenectady Sub-District 2 CCC Yearbook for 1936; CCC Alumni website (www.cccalumni.org), NYS Office of Parks, Recreation and Historic Preservation; US Department of Agriculture/Natural Resources Conservation Service

CHAPTER NOTES

Chapter 1

1. Gifford Pinchot, letter to FDR, Jan. 20, 1933, FDR Presidential Library.
2. Nelson Brown, "The President Practices Forestry," Journal of Forestry, Feb. 1943.
3. Nelson Brown, "The President's Christmas Trees," Journal of Forestry, Dec. 1941.
4. Franklin D. Roosevelt, memo to Mr. Plog, Oct. 18, 1943, FDR National Historic Site Archives.
5. John Solan, "Nursing Forests Back to Health," The Conservationist, Feb. 2003.
6. Cabell Phillips, New York Times Chronicle of American Life, 1929–39, New York Times Co., 1969, 17.
7. "4-H Will Plant 40,000 Trees," Catskill Mountain News, March 10, 1933; "26,000 Trees Shipped into Greene County," Windham Journal, April 26, 1934; interview with Orville Slutzky, March 28, 2008.
8. "School Forest for Walton," Walton Reporter, Sept. 20, 1924.
9. Helen Lane, The Story of Walton, 1785–1975, 159.
10. Norman Van Valkenburgh, "The John Burroughs Memorial Forest," Catskill Center News, Summer 1985.
11. Bernard Bellush, FDR as Governor of New York, Columbia University Press, 1955, 94–95.
12. Ibid., 98.

Chapter 2

1. Phillips, 34–35.
2. Ibid., 45.
3. Encyclopedia of New York State, Syracuse University Press, 2005, 1543.
4. Ibid.
5. Phillips, 75.
6. T. H. Watkins, The Great Depression, America in the 1930s, Blackside Inc., 1933.

Chapter 3

1. John Salmond, The Civilian Conservation Corps 1933–1942, A New Deal Case Study, Duke University Press, 1967, 8.
2. Gifford Pinchot, letter to FDR, Jan. 20, 1933, FDR Presidential Library.
3. Perry H. Merrill, Roosevelt's Forest Army, A History of the Civilian Conservation Corps 1933–1942, Montpelier, VT, 1981, 196.
4. "With the Civilian Conservation Corps," American Forests, July 1933.
5. Robert Fechner, memorandum, "Private Lands," April 18, 1933, FDR Presidential Library.
6. "With the Civilian Conservation Corps," American Forests, July 1933.

Chapter 4

1. Camp Inspection Report, Aug, 8, 1933, National Archives.
2. Interview with Herb Glass, Feb. 9, 2004.
3. Interview with Merlin DuBois, Feb. 15, 2007.
4. Mitch Keller, "Roots, The Legacy of the CCC," Ulster Magazine, Winter 1996.
5. Camp Inspection Report, Aug. 8, 1933.
6. Interview with Ed Ocker, Feb. 17, 2007.
7. Interview with Bud Eckert, Feb. 11, 2007.
8. Camp Inspection Report, Aug. 7, 1933.
9. "Library Notes," Camp Wienecke News, Mar. 7, 1935.
10. Happy Days, Oct. 3, 1934.
11. "Call for Winter Sports Finds Many Candidates," Happy Days, undated.
12. Interview with LeRoy Winchell, Feb. 8, 2004.
13. Interview with Bud Eckert, Feb. 11, 2007.
14. Charles Taylor, letter to Margaret Roeh, Apr. 18, 1934.
15. "CCC Men Sign Pay Releases," Oneonta Daily Star, April 1935.

16. "New Names Put on Relief Rolls," *Oneonta Daily Star*, Mar. 18, 1935.

17. "Communications," *Camp Wienecke News*, Mar. 7, 1935.

18. Second Corps Area Newsletter 1, June 7, 1935.

19. Correspondence between McIntee and Granger, April 2, April 4, June 3, 1935.

20. Second Corps Area Newsletter #14, Oct. 7, 1935.

21. "Boiceville Conservation Camp Ordered Closed on January 1," *Kingston Freeman*, Dec. 21, 1935.

22. G. A. Moore, memo to Second Corps Area Commanders, Dec. 28, 1935.

23. Interview with Bud Eckert, Feb. 11, 2007.

Chapter 5

1. "US Forest Camp in Delaware Has Crew of Happy Workers," untitled clipping, June 27, 1933.

2. "More Men Arrive at Forest Camps," *Oneonta Daily Star*, June 26, 1933.

3. "Davenport CCC Camp Organized," *Oneonta Daily Star*, July 7, 1933.

4. "Flag Raising Ceremony Plan at CCC Camp," *Oneonta Daily Star*, July 22, 1933.

5. "Flag Donated for Civilian Conservation Corps Camp," *Oneonta Daily Star*, July 15, 1933.

6. "CCC Making Good Progress," *Oneonta Daily Star*, Aug. 23, 1933.

7. Martin Podskoch, *Fire Towers of the Catskills, Their History and Lore*, Purple Mountain Press, 2000, 82.

8. "State Completes New Steel Tower Atop Utsayantha," *Stamford Mirror-Recorder*, July 26, 1934.

9. Podskoch, 78.

10. NYS Conservation Department, Annual Report to the Legislature, 1936, 140.

11. "Roosevelt Greets Workers in Camps by Radio," *Forestry News Digest*, August 1933, FDR Presidential Library.

Chapter 6

1. *Bugs & Blisters*, August 9, 1934.

2. *Deposit Courier*, May 16, 1935.

3. Camp Inspection Report, March. 28, 1934.

4. "Contingent of CCC Workers at West End Camp," *Deposit Courier*, Nov. 16, 1933.

5. "The Parting of Friends," *Bugs & Blisters*, Sept. 1934.

6. Camp Inspection Reports, Mar. 28, 1934, May 6, 1935.

7. *Bugs & Blisters*, Nov. 9, 1934.

8. "Forestry Notes," *Bugs & Blisters*, Sept. 20, 1935.

9. *Bugs & Blisters*, Nov. 9, 1934.

10. *Deposit Courier*, July 26, 1934 and Aug. 6, 1934; Bugs & Blisters, Dec. 10, 1934.

11. Podskoch, 89.

12. *Bugs & Blisters*, Sept. 20, 1935.

13. "Red Cross Relief for 3,000 Families in New York State Floods," *Delaware Express*, July 26, 1935.

14. "Officials Compliment Men of McClure CCC for Flood Relief Work," *Deposit Courier*, Aug. 8, 1935.

15. *Happy Days*, July 7, 1934; *Bugs & Blisters*, Oct. 1934.

16. "Superintendent's Column," *Bugs & Blisters*, Dec. 10, 1934.

17. *Happy Days*, Sept. 1, 1934.

18. Camp Inspection Report, May 6, 1935.

19. "Turn Camp Over to Army," *Oneonta Daily Star*, Dec. 12, 1936.

20. Conversation with Ed Engelman, January 2008.

Chapter 7

1. Podskoch, 31.

2. Roland Van Zandt, *The Catskill Mountain House*, Black Dome Press, Hensonville, NY, 1991, 305.

3. Schenectady Sub-District 2 CCC Yearbook, 1936, 85.

4. NYS Conservation Dept. Annual Report to the Legislature, 1934, 101.

5. Michael Kudish, *The Catskill Forest: A History*, Purple Mountain Press, Fleischmanns, NY, 2000, 119.

6. H. A. Haring, *Our Catskill Mountains*, G. P. Putnam's Sons, NY, 1931, 254.

7. John Ham, Robert Bucenec, *Light Rails and Short Ties through the Notch, The Stony Clove and Catskill Mountain Railroad*, Stony Clove and Catskill Mountain Press, Hunter, NY, 2002.

8. Schenectady Sub-District 2 CCC Yearbook, 1936, 85; NYS Conservation Dept. Annual Report to the Legislature, 1937.

9. "Company 291 Has Gone through Many Varied Experiences," *Tannersville Tiger*, June 23, 1934.

10. Camp Inspection Reports, May 23, 1934 and Apr. 2, 1935.

11. "Name Camp for Rip Van Winkle in Big Day's Celebration," *Happy Days*, July 21, 1934.

12. NYS Conservation Dept. Annual Report to the Legislature, 1936.

13. *Happy Days*, various articles, 1934.

14. Camp Inspection Report, April 6, 1935.

15. Ibid.

16. Schenectady Sub-District 2 CCC Yearbook, 1936, 84.

17. Interview with William Reich, 2004.

Chapter 8

1. "I Guess I Can Take It," *The Advance*, Oct. 1934.

2. Interview with Phil Skowfoe, 2006.

3. "Construction of 15 Buildings in County CCC Camp Finished," unidentified newspaper clipping in scrapbook, Middleburgh Historical Society archives.

4. "Plan CCC Camp at Breakabeen," *Stamford Mirror-Recorder*, Mar. 29, 1934.

5. "CCC Camps Plant 8 Million Trees," *Oneonta Daily Star*, Apr. 6, 1937.

6. *Schenectady Gazette* article, April 14,

1938, scrapbook, FDR Presidential Library.

7. Mitch Keller, "Roots, The Legacy of the CCC," *Ulster Magazine*, Winter 1996.

8. Podskoch, 79, 86.

9. Interview with John Jankowski, Nov. 23, 2007.

10. Biography of Donald E. Dietz, provided by Ruth Dietz, 2004.

11. Interview with Helen Effner Irving, 2006.

12. Unidentified newspaper article, 1983.

13. Lester E. Hendrix, *Slaughters History of Schoharie County*, Schoharie County NY Historical Society, 1994, 206.

14. *Delaware Express*, Jan. 4, Feb. 1, 1935; Schoharie County Supreme Court records.

15. Schenectady Sub-District 2 CCC Yearbook, 1936.

16. "Two Breakabeen Camp Men to be Honored Friday," *Middleburgh News*, May 18, 1939.

17. "Storm Damage," *Middleburgh News*, Sept. 29, 1938; Report of Special Inspector, May 20, 1940.

18. Letter from Ross Abare, Special Investigator, to Charles Kenlan, June 22, 1938, and other CCC communications and inspection reports, 1937–1940, National Archives.

19. "Breakabeen Wins CCC Track Meet," *Middleburgh News*, Oct. 6, 1938.

20. Camp Educational Report, Aug. 10, 1939.

21. Camp Inspection Report, Mar. 20, 1941.

22. Interview with John Jankowski, Nov. 23, 2007.

Chapter 9

1. *Catskill Mountain News*, Aug. 9, Oct. 25, Nov. 1, 1935.

2. Ibid.

3. "CCC Camp Will Improve Entire Region," *Catskill Mountain News*, June 7, 1935.

4. "Many Projects for Summer at Local Camp," *Catskill Mountain News*, April 3, 1936.

5. NYS Conservation Dept. Annual Report to the Legislature, 1938, 129.

6. Interviews with Lester Rosa, 2004, 2008.

7. "Orders Changed, CCC Camp to Stay in This Village," *Catskill Mountain News*, May 27, 1936.

8. Schenectady Sub-District 2 CCC Yearbook, 1936.

9. Cultural Resources Investigation of Beaverkill Public Campground, NYS DEC, July 30, 1990.

10. NYS Conservation Dept. Annual Reports to the Legislature, 1926–28.

11. Haring, 255.

12. *Catskill Mountain News*, June 7, 1935.

13. Correspondence, Sept. 28, Oct. 7, 1936.

14. Schenectady Sub-District 2 CCC Yearbook, 1936.

15. Interview with Hank Geary, Nov. 1, 2004.

16. "Local CCC Camp Not to Disband," *Catskill Mountain News*, Sept. 24, 1937.

17. Interview with Stanton Hogan, Jan. 24, 2004.

18. Interviews with Leonard Utter, Lester Rosa, Michael Kudish.

19. Interview with Bob Reed, Jan. 15, 2007.

20. "Camp Has Reading Room," *Catskill Mountain News*, Aug. 26, 1938.

21. *Catskill Mountain News*, April 1, 1938.

22. Interview with Howard Etts Jr., Jan. 12, 2004.

23. "CCC Camp Will Play Basketball," *Catskill Mountain News*, Jan. 31, 1936.

Chapter 10

1. Norman Van Valkenburgh, *Land Acquisition for New York State, An Historical Perspective*, 119–20.

2. Camp Inspection Reports, July 21, 1934 and May 6, 1935.

3. Camp Inspection Report, July 21, 1934.

4. Ibid.

5. Map, hand-drawn by Russ Gundelach, 1992.

6. "What Masonville CCC Has Done since Start," *Unadilla Times*, Jan. 1, 1936; "Achievements of Work Projects at Camp S-100," *Deposit Record*, Nov. 21, 1935.

7. "Compliments for Boys of CCC Camp," *Catskill Mountain News*, July 26, 1935.

8. *Sidney Record*, Oct. 10, 1935 and Dec. 10, 1935.

9. "299th Co. CCC to Sponsor Dinner Dance," *Sidney Record*, Nov. 15, 1934; "CCC Camps Get Snow Plows," *Sidney Record*, Feb. 1, 1935.

10. Interview with Red Charles, Jan. 24, 2004.

11. NYS Conservation Dept. Annual Reports to the Legislature, 1936–41.

12. Forest Service Work Report, U.S. Dept. of Agriculture, Aug. 1, 1939.

13. Report of Special Investigator Patrick King, May 14, 1940; Memo to CCC Director from Representative on CCC Advisory Council, June 22, 1940.

14. Russ Gundelach, letter to Sanford Shelton, Dec. 21, 1992.

15. "CCC Boys Remember Doctor Danforth," letter to the editor from Dominick August, *Tri-Town News*, Oct. 9, 1996.

16. Interview with Dominick August, Feb. 13, 2004.

Chapter 11

1. Salmond, 210.

2. List of CCC Camp Superintendents, Jan. 1, 1942, NYS Conservation Dept. Personnel Records.

3. Franklin D. Roosevelt, letter to James McIntee, Mar. 25, 1942.

4. Salmond, 215–217.

5. NYS Conservation Dept. Annual Report to the Legislature, 1942.

6. Ibid.

BIBLIOGRAPHY

Books

Beasley, Maurine, et al, editors. *Eleanor Roosevelt Encyclopedia*. Westport, CT: Greenwood Press, 2001.

Belush, Bernard. *FDR as Governor of New York*. New York: Columbia University Press, 1955.

Briggs, Mary S. *Davenport, Fact and Fiction*. Davenport, NY: Davenport Historical Society, 2004.

Cohen, Stan. *The Tree Army, A Pictorial History of the Civilian Conservation Corps 1933–1942*. Missoula, MT: Pictorial Histories Publishing Co., 1980.

Dickson, Paul, and Thomas B. Allen. *The Bonus Army, An American Epic*. New York: Walker Publishing Co., 2004.

Eisenstadt, Peter, editor in chief. *Encyclopedia of New York State*. Syracuse, NY: Syracuse University Press, 2005.

Evers, Alf. *The Catskills, From Wilderness to Woodstock*. Woodstock, NY: Overlook Press, 1982.

Godwin, Doris Kearns. *No Ordinary Time, Franklin and Eleanor Roosevelt: The Homefront in World War II*. New York: Simon & Schuster, 1994.

Ham, John M., and Robert Bucenec. *Light Rails and Short Ties through the Notch, The Stony Clove and Catskill Mountain Railroad and Her Steam Legacy*. Hunter, NY: Stony Clove and Catskill Mountain Press, 2002.

Haring, H. A. *Our Catskill Mountains*. New York: G. P. Putnam's Sons, 1931.

Hendrix, Lester E. *Slaughters History of Schoharie County*. Schoharie, NY: Schoharie County Historical Society, 1994.

Hill, Edwin G. *In the Shadow of the Mountain, The Spirit of the Civilian Conservation Corps*. Pullman, WA: Washington State University, 1990.

Kiefer, E. Kay, and Paul Fellows. *Hobnail Boots and Khaki Suits*. Chicago, IL: Adams Press, 1983.

Kudish, Michael. *The Catskill Forest: A History*. Fleischmanns, NY: Purple Mountain Press, 2000.

Lane, Helen. *The Story of Walton, 1785–1975, by Many of Its People*. Walton, NY: Walton Historical Society, 1975.

Malatsky, David M. *Summer Camp! The History of the New York City Summer Camps, from Hunter's Island to Ten Mile River, 1910–2002*. New York: Greater New York Councils, 2002.

Mankiller, Wilma Pearl, et al, editors. *Reader's Companion to US Women's History*. Boston, MA: Houghton Mifflin, 1998.

McElvaine, Robert, editor. *Down and Out in the Great Depression, Letters from the Forgotten Man*. Chapel Hill, NC: University of North Carolina Press, 1983.

Merrill, Perry H. *Roosevelt's Forest Army, A History of the Civilian Conservation Corps 1933–1942*. Montpelier, VT: Perry Merrill, 1984.

Newton, Norman T. *Design on the Land, The Development of Landscape Architecture*. Cambridge, MA: Belknap Press of Harvard University Press, 1971.

Official Annual, Schenectady District Civilian Conservation Corps, Second Corps Area. Schenectady, NY: CCC District Headquarters, 1937.

Phillips, Cabell. *From the Crash to the Blitz 1929–1939, the New York Times Chronicle of American Life*. New York: New York Times Co., 1969.

Pinchot, Gifford. *Breaking New Ground*. New York: Harcourt Brace & Co., 1947.

Podskoch, Martin. *Fire Towers of the Catskills, Their History and Lore*. Fleischmanns, NY: Purple Mountain Press, 2000.

Salmond, John. *The Civilian Conservation Corps 1933–1942, A New Deal Case Study*. Durham, NC: Duke University Press, 1967.

Scott, Phil. *Hemingway's Hurricane, The Great Florida Keys Storm of 1935.* Camden, ME: International Marine/McGraw Hill, 2006.

Terkel, Studs. *Hard Times, An Oral History of the Great Depression.* New York: Pantheon Books, 1970.

Van Valkenburgh, Norman. *Land Acquisition for New York State, An Historical Perspective.* Arkville, NY: Catskill Center for Conservation & Development, 1985.

Van Zandt, Roland. *The Catskill Mountain House.* Hensonville, NY: Black Dome Press, 1991.

Watkins, T. H. *The Great Depression, America in the 1930s.* Boston, MA: Blackside, Inc., 1993.

Williams, George W. *The USDA Forest Service, the First Century.* Washington, DC: USDA Forest Service, 2000.

Articles

Brown, Nelson C. "The President Practices Forestry." *Journal of Forestry.* Feb. 1943.

———. "The President's Christmas Trees." *American Forests.* Dec. 1941.

Goodman, David. "The Skiing Legacy of the CCC." *Ski Magazine.* Dec. 1994.

Keller, Mitch. "Roots, The Legacy of the CCC." *Ulster Magazine.* Winter 1996.

Meyer, George. "Rip Van Winkle Awoke in 1935." *Tannersville Topics.* Circa 1938.

McIntee, James. "The CCC and National Defense." *American Forests.* July 1940.

"Millions of Years in the Making, A Century of State Stewardship." *The Preservationist.* Spring/Summer 2006.

"New York's Heartland, Development of the State Parks Program in Central New York 1925–50. *New York Preservationist.* n.d.

Patton, Thomas. "FDR's Trees." *The Conservationist.* April 1995.

———. "'What of Her?' Eleanor Roosevelt and Camp TERA." *New York History.* Spring 2006.

"Roosevelt Greets Workers in Camps by Radio." *Forestry News Digest.* August 1933.

Solon, John. "Nursing Forests Back to Health." *The Conservationist.* February 2003.

Speakman, Joseph. "Into the Woods, The First Year of the CCC." *Prologue.* Fall 2006.

Swing, Raymond. "Take the Army out of the CCC." *The Nation.* Oct. 23, 1935.

Teasdale, Parry. "Done for Fun, Mickey Simpson Recalls New York's First Ski Slope." *Woodstock Times.* Dec. 1, 1988.

Van Valkenburgh, Norman. "The John Burroughs Memorial Forest." *Catskill Center News.* Summer 1985.

———. "One More Centennial to Go." *Adirondac.* July/Aug. 1995.

Verschoor, Karin. "A Century of Seedlings, DEC's Saratoga Nursery." *The Conservationist.* Oct. 2007.

"With the CCC." *American Forests.* July 1933.

Newspapers

Catskill Mountain News. Fairview Public Library, Margaretville.

Delaware Express. Cannon Free Library, Delhi.

Deposit Courier. Deposit Free Library.

Kingston Daily Freeman. Kingston Area Library.

Middleburgh News. Middleburgh Public Library.

Oneonta Daily Star. Huntington Library, Oneonta.

Stamford Mirror-Recorder. Stamford Library.

Tri-Town News. Sidney Historical Society.

Windham Journal. Windham Journal, Windham

Camp Newspapers

The Advance (Breakabeen)

Bugs & Blisters (McClure; Deposit Library)

Camp Wienecke News (Boiceville)

Cold Springer (Masonville)

Foxes' Tales (Gallupville; Old Stone Fort Museum, Schoharie)

Happy Days (National CCC)

The Tiger (Tannersville; Vedder Memorial Library, Coxsackie)

Records Repositories

Catskills Oral History Archives. Catskill Center for Conservation & Development, Arkville, NY.

Franklin Delano Roosevelt Presidential Library (FDR Personal and Official Files; Louis Howe File), Hyde Park, NY.

Home of Franklin D. Roosevelt National Historic Site Archives (FDR and Forestry), National Park Service, Hyde Park, NY.

New York State Conservation Department Annual Reports to the Legislature, 1926–1942, including A Biological Survey of the Delaware & Susquehanna Watersheds Supplement to the 25th Annual Report, 1935. New York State Library, Albany, NY.

New York State Conservation Department, CCC Camp and Personnel Files,1933–42. New York State Archives, Albany, NY.

New York State Department of Environmental Conservation, Division of Lands & Forests files. Region III headquarters, New Paltz, NY.

Records of Civilian Conservation Corps 1933–1953 (Record Group 35—camp files). National Archives and Records Administration, College Park, MD.

Online Sources

A Brief History of the NYS Forest Program. www.dec.ny.gov/lands/4982.html

The Civilian Conservation Corps Legacy (formerly National Association of Civilian Conservation Corps Alumni). www.ccca-lumni.org

The Civilian Conservation Corps and the National Park Service 1933–42, An Administrative History. www.nps.gov/history/history/online_books/ccc

History of the Florida Keys Memorial. www.keyshistory.org/hurrmemorial html

James F. Justin Civilian Conservation Corps Museum. http://members.aol com/famjustin/ccchis.html

New York State Civilian Conservation Corps Museum at Gilbert Lake State Park. www.nyscccmuseum.com

INDEX

ABOUT THE AUTHOR

 Diane Galusha has written several books of local and regional history, including *Liquid Assets, The Story of New York City's Water System* (1999, Purple Mountain Press), *Through a Woman's Eye: Pioneering Photographers of Rural Upstate* (1991, Black Dome Press), *When Cauliflower was King* (2004, Purple Mountain Press), and *As the River Runs, A History of Halcottsville, N.Y.* (1990, self-published).

The founding president of the Historical Society of the Town of Middletown, she is also deeply involved in promoting the legacy of John Burroughs through preservation of Woodchuck Lodge, the literary naturalist's Roxbury summer home.

Diane is a former journalist and newspaper editor, currently employed at the Catskill Watershed Corporation in Margaretville. She has been a grateful resident of the Catskills since 1982.